Quiz Night

You won't need to phone a friend

Collins

HarperCollins Publishers
Westerhill Road, Glasgow G64 2QT

The Collins website is www.collins.co.uk

Collins New Quiz Book first published 2000
Collins New Quiz Book 2 first published 2002
This compilation first published 2004

© HarperCollins Publishers 2004

Reprint 5

ISBN 0 00 719525 7

A catalogue record for this book is available from the British Library

Typeset by Davidson Pre-Press Graphics Ltd, Glasgow

Printed and bound in Great Britain by Clays Ltd, St Ives plc

CONTENTS

How TO USE THIS BOOK

In *Collins Quiz Night*, each double-page spread comprises a numbered set of twelve multiple-choice questions; the answers to each set are given in the vertical panel on the right-hand page of the following double-page spread. This panel is numbered to show the set to which it contains the answers. For example, the questions of Set 1 are on pages 6 and 7 while the answers are on page 9 – the idea is that you only have to turn a page to find the answers.

So, have fun and good luck!

Q U E S T I O N S I

1 Who is the Toytown garage-owner in Enid Blyton's *Noddy* stories?

  A Mr Sparks
  B Mr Spanner
  C Mr Skid

2 In the film *Interview With The Vampire*, who played the vampire being interviewed?

  A Tom Cruise
  B Brad Pitt
  C Christian Slater

3 What or who was St Patrick believed to have expelled from Ireland?

  A The English
  B Snakes
  C Demons

4 If you were in the city of Winnipeg, which of Canada's provinces would you be in?

  A Alberta
  B Manitoba
  C Saskatchewan

5 If you suffered from androphobia, what would you be afraid of?

  A Men
  B Men called Andrew
  C Androids

6 In cricket, what does it mean if the umpire raises his forefinger to the batsman?

  A He is allowing him one run
  B He is calling him out
  C He is telling him off

7 What task were corgi dogs specially bred for?

    A Tripping up burglars
    B Herding sheep
    C Carrying messages

8 What big advance was made in television in the UK in 1967?

    A The first-ever Queen's Christmas message
    B The first-ever Match of the Day
    C The first-ever colour TV broadcast

9 What song was used by the Labour Party as its General Election campaign song in 1997?

    A *Things Can Only Get Better*
    B *The Drugs Don't Work*
    C *Come On You Reds*

10 What is the connection between the sitcom *Till Death Us Do Part* and Tony Blair?

    A Tony Blair's father wrote the series
    B Tony Blair's father-in-law was a series regular
    C Tony Blair was a child actor in the show

11 How did commander Jim Lovell communicate that Apollo 13 had mechanical difficulties?

    A Oh, shoot
    B You won't believe what Jack's just done
    C Houston, we have a problem

12 What Blue Peter regular was found to have been a different sex than originally thought?

    A John Noakes
    B Shep the dog
    C Fred the tortoise

1 On a standard typewriter keyboard, which vowel does NOT appear on the top line of letters?

   A O
   B A
   C E

2 In polo, what is a chukka?

   A The person who throws in the ball to start
   B One of the periods when play goes on
   C The type of ponies that are used

3 What US state is represented by the initials Ia?

   A Indiana
   B Idaho
   C Iowa

4 A star of *Buffy The Vampire Slayer* featured in a popular series of British TV ads; for what?

   A Renault (Papa & Nicole series)
   B BT (Beattie series)
   C Gold Blend Coffee (Lovers' series)

5 What does the Statue of Liberty hold in her right hand?

   A An American flag
   B A torch
   C A tablet inscribed with the date of independence

6 What currency would you need in Vietnam?

   A Sum
   B Won
   C Dong

7 Mandela got out of jail, Iraq invaded Kuwait and Germany was reunified. What year was it?

   A 1990
   B 1991
   C 1992

8 Which butcher's son rose to power in Tudor England and built Hampton Court as his home?

   A Thomas Wolsey
   B Thomas Cromwell
   C Thomas Cranmer

9 What colour do Sikh brides wear on their wedding day?

   A White
   B Red
   C Yellow

10 Who usually occupies the nave in a church?

   A The choir
   B The priest
   C The congregation

11 Which of the following does an ISO rating classify?

   A Photographic film speed
   B Wind speed
   C Atmospheric humidity

12 What priceless find was discovered buried at Sutton Hoo in Suffolk?

   A An intact dinosaur skeleton
   B An Anglo-Saxon ship burial
   C A complete Roman temple

A

1
1	A
2	B
3	B
4	B
5	A
6	B
7	B
8	C
9	A
10	B
11	C
12	C

1 Who runs the Kwik-E-Mart in *The Simpsons*?

A Moe
B Apu
C Barney

---

2 On what film set did Lauren Bacall first meet Humphrey Bogart?

A *The Big Sleep*
B *Key Largo*
C *To Have And Have Not*

---

3 Who founded the Volkswagen company in 1937?

A Otto Volkswagen
B Germany's Nazi Government
C Ferdinand Porsche

---

4 What do the mistral, the sirocco and the monsoon have in common?

A They are winds
B They are rivers
C They are weather fronts

---

5 What is the RoSPA?

A Royal Society for the Protection of Animals
B Royal Society for the Prevention of Accidents
C Royal Society for the Promotion of the Arts

---

6 Who was Jackie Paper's childhood playmate?

A Puff, the Magic Dragon
B Rupert the Bear
C Nellie the Elephant

7 What school was Billy Bunter a pupil of?

    A St Custard's
    B The Remove
    C Greyfriars

8 In women's gymnastics, the four events are floor, beam, asymmetric bars … and what else?

    A Vaulting horse
    B Pommel horse
    C Rings

9 What day does Mardi Gras come before?

    A Shrove Tuesday
    B Ash Wednesday
    C Good Friday

10 Which of the Spice Girls first became a Spice mum?

    A Mel B
    B Mel C
    C Victoria

11 Who wrote the book that the movie *The Godfather* was based on?

    A Francis Ford Coppola
    B Mario Puzo
    C Leon Uris

12 How many Formula One championships did Jackie Stewart win?

    A 2
    B 3
    C 5

A 2

1	B
2	B
3	C
4	C
5	B
6	C
7	A
8	A
9	B
10	C
11	A
12	B

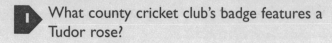

1 What county cricket club's badge features a Tudor rose?

    A Yorkshire
    B Northamptonshire
    C Lancashire

2 In the song *The Devil Went Down To Georgia*, how did the devil compete to win souls?

    A In card games
    B In fiddle contests
    C In dancing contests

3 What would a Scot do with an ashet?

    A Clean a coal fire with it
    B Put food in it
    C Wear it on the head

4 What Canadian maritime province was the home of *Anne of Green Gables*?

    A Nova Scotia
    B New Brunswick
    C Prince Edward Island

5 What British commander was responsible for the long attrition on the Western Front in WWI?

    A *John French*
    B *Douglas Haig*
    C *H. H. Kitchener*

6 What girl group did Louise Nurding first come to fame with?

    A Shakespeare's Sister
    B Eternal
    C Bananarama

7 What element is there more of than any other in the earth's crust?

    A Hydrogen
    B Iron
    C Oxygen

8 Whose Ford Gran Torino was called The Striped Tomato?

    A Kojak
    B Starsky & Hutch
    C Bodie & Doyle

9 What is the smallest country in the world?

    A Vatican State
    B San Marino
    C Monaco

10 For how long did Victoria reign over us?

    A 63 years
    B 61 years
    C 59 years

11 Who played Rosemary in *Rosemary's Baby*?

    A Sharon Tate
    B Twiggy
    C Mia Farrow

12 What well-known socialist couple founded the LSE?

    A Sidney & Beatrice Webb
    B Thomas & Jane Carlyle
    C William Blake & Catherine Boucher

A

3

1 B
2 C
3 B
4 A
5 B
6 A
7 C
8 A
9 B
10 A
11 B
12 B

1 Who was the first Emperor of Rome?

   A Julius Caesar
   B Claudius
   C Augustus

2 What Disney animated film features the song *You've Got A Friend In Me*?

   A *Toy Story*
   B *Aladdin*
   C *Beauty and the Beast*

3 What was unique about American President David Riche Atchison?

   A He was president for only 24 hours
   B He was assassinated before his inauguration
   C He declined the office after his election

4 In what sport would you expect to find a shortstop?

   A Formula One motor racing
   B Croquet
   C Baseball

5 What is the square root of 36?

   A 3
   B 6
   C 12

6 Which character 'spoke' the narrator's voice-overs in *The Waltons*?

   A Ike Godsey
   B John Boy
   C Gran'pa Walton

7 What nationality was South American guerrilla leader Che Guevara?

   A Bolivian
   B Cuban
   C Argentinian

8 Who didn't need this *Fascist Groove Thang* in 1981, and again in 1993?

   A Heaven 17
   B Fun Boy Three
   C Fine Young Cannibals

9 What is St Matthew the patron saint of?

   A Social outcasts
   B Tax officials
   C Writers

10 What spirit is the main ingredient for the cocktails Tom Collins, Pink Lady and Sloe Screw?

   A White rum
   B Gin
   C Vodka

11 What is vellum parchment made from?

   A Calf skin
   B Reed fibres
   C Tree bark

12 What were the names of the two rival pigs in *George Orwell's Animal Farm*?

   A Napoleon and Wellington
   B Napoleon and Snowball
   C Napoleon and Josephine

A
4

1 **B**
2 **B**
3 **B**
4 **C**
5 **B**
6 **B**
7 **C**
8 **B**
9 **A**
10 **A**
11 **C**
12 **A**

15

1 What is the next number in the sequence: 49, 64, 81...

    A 98
    B 100
    C 106

2 Which of the following is not a province of Ireland?

    A Ulster
    B Connacht
    C Louth

3 What is a close encounter of the first kind?

    A Sighting a UFO
    B Finding physical evidence left by a UFO
    C Sighting or physical contact with an alien

4 In American slang, if you were wearing cheaters, what would you have on?

    A False eyelashes
    B Glasses
    C High-heeled shoes

5 Who had a top 10 hit in 1998 with *Mulder & Scully*?

    A Catatonia
    B Ace of Base
    C Manic Street Preachers

6 What English football club's nickname is the *Tykes*?

    A Millwall
    B Barnsley
    C Grimsby Town

7 What was launched on the 40th anniversary of the Russian Revolution?

    A The battleship Potemkin
    B The Sputnik satellite
    C The USSR's new fleet of nuclear-powered subs

8 Homer's ancient Greek classics *The Iliad & The Odyssey* provided inspiration for what musical?

    A *By Jupiter*
    B *A Funny Thing Happened on the Way to the Forum*
    C *The Golden Apple*

9 Who had a top 40 hit in 1980 called *New Amsterdam*?

    A Graham Parker & The Rumour
    B Elvis Costello
    C Billy Bragg

10 What fair did Uncle Tom Cobbleigh and all want to get to?

    A Winchester
    B Widdicombe
    C Windermere

11 What was Archibald Leach better known as?

    A Kirk Douglas
    B Cary Grant
    C Gary Cooper

12 What was the name of the *Thunderbirds'* ex-con chauffeur who drove a pink Rolls-Royce?

    A Brains
    B Lady Penelope
    C Parker

A 5	
1	C
2	A
3	A
4	C
5	B
6	B
7	C
8	A
9	B
10	B
11	A
12	B

17

1 Before going solo, what all-girl band did Belinda Carlisle front?

A The Bangles
B The Go-Gos
C Vixen

2 Juno, Queen of the Roman gods, derived from what equivalent Greek goddess?

A Hera
B Athene
C Aphrodite

3 What was the Duke of Wellington's own name?

A John Moore
B Arthur Wellesley
C Thomas Cochrane

4 What city was once known as Byzantium and then as Constantinople?

A Istanbul
B Baghdad
C Damascus

5 What is the collective term for a group of kangaroos?

A A boxing
B A troop
C A didgeridoo

6 Three of the four elements are earth, air and water; what is the fourth?

A Wind
B Fire
C The Heavens

7 Where are the Slough of Despond, the Valley of the Shadow of Death and the Celestial City?

A In the *Book of Mormon*
B In *The Pilgrim's Progress*
C In *The Bible*

8 What racecourse hosts the classic St Leger?

A Ascot
B Doncaster
C Aintree

9 Whose brain starred in the long-running *Spitting Image* sketch, The President's Brain Is Missing?

A Richard Nixon's
B John F. Kennedy's
C Ronald Reagan's

10 Who had a number 2 hit in 1990 with the operatic aria *Nessun Dorma*?

A Placido Domingo
B José Carreras
C Luciano Pavarotti

11 Who was the only British Prime Minister ever to be assassinated?

A Spencer Percival
B Robert Walpole
C William Pitt

12 If you went to see a horse opera, what would you be watching?

A A showjumping display
B A western movie
C A horseracing meeting

A

6

1	B
2	C
3	A
4	B
5	A
6	B
7	B
8	C
9	B
10	B
11	B
12	C

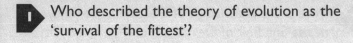

1 Who described the theory of evolution as the 'survival of the fittest'?

    A T. H. Huxley
    B Charles Darwin
    C Herbert Spencer

2 Which planet is second from the sun?

    A Mars
    B Mercury
    C Venus

3 Manchester U., Liverpool and Arsenal won the double in the 20th century. What other team did?

    A Leeds Utd
    B Tottenham Hotspur
    C Newcastle Utd

4 What was the name of the Cartwrights' ranch in the long-running TV western show *Bonanza*?

    A Ponderosa
    B The Big C
    C The High Chapparal

5 What is gymnophobia a fear of?

    A Gymnasiums
    B Nudity
    C Getting undressed for physical exercise

6 The world's shortest play is a 35-second, dialogue-free effort by Samuel Beckett. What is it called?

    A *Blink*
    B *Breath*
    C *Blast*

7 What is the translation of the title of Enrique Iglesias' hit, *Bailamos*?

   A Rhythm Is Everything
   B I Want You
   C Let's Dance

8 What did Georgie Porgie do when the boys came out?

   A Played with them
   B Ran away
   C Cried

9 What does the Italian word 'opera' mean?

   A Stories
   B Work
   C Songs

10 Metal-toothed villain Jaws appeared in two Bond films. *Moonraker* was one; what was the other?

   A *The Spy Who Loved Me*
   B *Octopussy*
   C *For Your Eyes Only*

11 What American state's nickname is Land of Enchantment?

   A California
   B New Mexico
   C Hawaii

12 What street did the Great Fire of London start in?

   A Chandlers Lane
   B Brick Lane
   C Pudding Lane

A

7

1	B
2	A
3	B
4	A
5	B
6	B
7	B
8	B
9	C
10	C
11	A
12	B

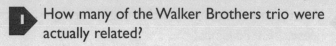

1 How many of the Walker Brothers trio were actually related?

    A All 3
    B 2
    C None

---

2 In *Dad's Army*, what was Private Fraser's catchphrase?

    A Doomed, I say … we're all doomed
    B They don't like it up 'em, they don't
    C Stupid boy

---

3 Who was Sirhan Sirhan's famous victim in the 1960s?

    A Martin Luther King
    B Bobby Kennedy
    C Malcolm X

---

4 What school of witchcraft and wizardry does Harry Potter attend?

    A Hogwarts
    B Durmstrang
    C Goblin's Hall

---

5 What animal name is given to Sirius, the brightest star?

    A The Dog Star
    B The Bear Star
    C The Lion Star

---

6 What is unique about the mythic bird the phoenix?

    A It is reborn in fire
    B It can swim in the sea
    C It has a magical horn on its head

7 What country first gave women the vote?

A New Zealand
B UK
C Portugal

8 How many points does a player score for a goal in hurling?

A 1
B 2
C 3

9 Which of the Twelve Apostles was replaced by Matthias?

A Judas Iscariot
B Peter
C Simon the Zealot

10 How did dinosaurs gestate their young?

A In sacs of mucus suspended from tree branches
B In eggs
C In shallow stagnant water

11 What do Aiguebelle, Centerbe and Ettaler have in common?

A They are French cheeses
B They are herbal liqueurs
C They are villages in Provence

12 Which movie do the main characters in *When Harry Met Sally* lie in bed watching?

A *Now Voyager*
B *Casablanca*
C *An Affair To Remember*

A

8

1 C
2 C
3 B
4 A
5 B
6 B
7 C
8 B
9 B
10 A
11 B
12 C

1 What do Britney Spears and Christina Aguilera have in common?

    A Both performed with the Mickey Mouse Club
    B Both fancy Prince William
    C Both went to the same school

2 If someone is an octogenarian, what decade of their life are they in?

    A Seventh
    B Eighth
    C Ninth

3 What writer was forced by his government to decline his Nobel Prize for literature?

    A Boris Pasternak
    B Alexander Solzhenitsyn
    C Jean-Paul Sartre

4 What solo singing star began his career with the Spencer Davis Group and Traffic?

    A Phil Collins
    B Eric Clapton
    C Steve Winwood

5 What natural feature occupies a quarter of Africa?

    A The Sahara Desert
    B The savanna grasslands
    C Water, in rivers, waterfalls and lakes

6 Which of the following did not rule the Holy Roman Empire?

    A Charles the Bald
    B Charles the Fat
    C Charles the Wise

7 In what sport did Bill Beaumont captain England?

    A Rugby league
    B Rugby union
    C Cricket

8 In the kitsch 70s series *Charlie's Angels*, what was unusual about Charlie?

    A He was a woman
    B He was never on screen
    C He was a villain

9 Who dreamed up the original Utopia?

    A Henry VIII
    B Thomas More
    C Cardinal Wolsey

10 In the movie *Back To The Future*, what speed must the car go at to travel through time?

    A 86 mph
    B 88 mph
    C 89 mph

11 What country are the Ozarks in?

    A Norway
    B USA
    C Russia

12 Moriarty was one of the great villains of literature. Who was his famous adversary?

    A Sherlock Holmes
    B Hercule Poirot
    C Sam Spade

A
9

1 C
2 A
3 B
4 A
5 A
6 A
7 A
8 C
9 A
10 B
11 B
12 B

1 Who is the wizard in *The Lord Of The Rings* trilogy?

    A Merlin
    B Gandalf
    C Taliesin

2 In professional boxing, what would a fighter weighing 140–147 pounds be called?

    A Welterweight
    B Lightweight
    C Flyweight

3 What actor, destined for stardom, played the corpse in the 1983 film *The Big Chill*?

    A Kevin Kline
    B Kevin Bacon
    C Kevin Costner

4 Roughly what speed would you be travelling at if you were in a boat doing 20 knots?

    A 15 mph
    B 19 mph
    C 23 mph

5 Who investigated the murdering headless horseman of *Sleepy Hollow*?

    A Rip Van Winkle
    B Ichabod Crane
    C Billy Budd

6 What TV show features the Cafe Nervosa?

    A *Friends*
    B *Frasier*
    C *Seinfeld*

7 What Joe Jackson song has the line 'Pretty women out walking with gorillas down my street'?

    A *Steppin' Out*
    B *It's Different For Girls*
    C *Is She Really Going Out With Him?*

8 How did Moses see God at Horeb, when He told him to lead the Israelites out of Egypt?

    A As a dark cloud with fire at the centre
    B As a shimmering golden cloud
    C As a burning bush

9 What plant does gin take its flavour from?

    A Juniper
    B Caraway
    C Angelica

10 Which of these wives outlived Henry VIII?

    A Catherine of Aragon
    B Catherine Howard
    C Catherine Parr

11 What is the second most spoken language in the world?

    A English
    B Chinese
    C Spanish

12 What UK actor won a Tony award in 1998 for his Broadway portrayal of the MC in *Cabaret*?

    A Richard E. Grant
    B Alan Cumming
    C Iain Glen

A 10

1	A
2	C
3	A
4	C
5	A
6	C
7	B
8	B
9	B
10	B
11	B
12	A

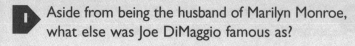

1 Aside from being the husband of Marilyn Monroe, what else was Joe DiMaggio famous as?

    A A newspaper reporter
    B A baseball player
    C A war hero

2 When was the United Nations founded?

    A 1918
    B 1945
    C 1953

3 Where will the 2006 World Cup be staged?

    A South Africa
    B Germany
    C England

4 What Kurt Weill opera, with the song *Mac The Knife*, was shut by the Nazis soon after opening?

    A *The Threepenny Opera*
    B *Rise And Fall Of The City Of Mahagonny*
    C *Street Scene*

5 What is the tune to Danny Boy also known as?

    A Princess Royal
    B The Derry Air
    C Lament for O'Carolan

6 What Shakespeare play was the inspiration for the film *Ten Things I Hate About You*?

    A *The Taming Of The Shrew*
    B *Much Ado About Nothing*
    C *Love's Labour's Lost*

7 If you wrote the number 600 in Roman numerals, what would you write?

    A DC
    B CCCCCC
    C WC

8 Who was Steed's first sidekick in *The Avengers*?

    A Tara King
    B Emma Peel
    C Cathy Gale

9 What boundary region has been long fought over by Israel and Syria?

    A The Sinai Peninsula
    B The West Bank
    C The Golan Heights

10 What Disney film featured the Bad 'Uns, Jasper and Horace?

    A *The Rescuers*
    B *101 Dalmatians*
    C *Pinocchio*

11 Before going solo, what pop group did Bryan Ferry front?

    A Roxy Music
    B Genesis
    C Dire Straits

12 What is a cor anglais?

    A A wildflower
    B A woodwind instrument
    C A custard pudding

1	B
2	A
3	C
4	C
5	B
6	B
7	C
8	C
9	A
10	C
11	A
12	B

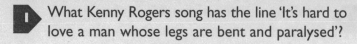
1 What Kenny Rogers song has the line 'It's hard to love a man whose legs are bent and paralysed'?

   A *Coward of the County*
   B *Ruby, Don't Take Your Love To Town*
   C *Lucille*

2 What name was given to foreigners who fought for the Spanish government in the Civil War?

   A The Socialist Brigade
   B The International Brigade
   C The Volunteer Brigade

3 Who invented the Mars Bar in 1920?

   A Frank Mars
   B Joe Barr
   C Joseph Rowntree

4 What does an Archimedes' Screw do?

   A Bores holes in rock
   B Lifts water
   C Calculates complex arithmetic problems

5 Where is the Ocean of Storms?

   A Antarctica
   B The South Atlantic
   C On the Moon

6 According to the Stranglers, what hero 'got an ice-pick that made his ears burn'?

   A Lenin
   B Trotsky
   C Stalin

7 What sport's name translates as 'the gentle way'?

    A Karate
    B Jujitsu
    C Judo

8 How many virtues were there traditionally thought to be?

    A 10
    B 7
    C 4

9 Who was the animator in *Monty Python's Flying Circus*?

    A Terry Gilliam
    B Terry Jones
    C Terry Thomas

10 What would you expect a cooper to make?

    A Carts
    B Barrels
    C Beer

11 Where is the priceless 8th-century Celtic illuminated manuscript *The Book of Kells* housed?

    A Dublin
    B Edinburgh
    C London

12 One of the two gangs in *West Side Story* was the Sharks; what was the other one?

    A Jeans
    B Jukes
    C Jets

1	B
2	B
3	B
4	A
5	B
6	A
7	A
8	C
9	C
10	B
11	A
12	B

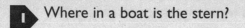

Q
U
E
S
T
I
O
N
S
14

1 Where in a boat is the stern?

A Front
B Rear
C Underside

2 Prince wrote the Bangles' first big hit. What was it?

A *Walk Like An Egyptian*
B *Eternal Flame*
C *Manic Monday*

3 Ingrid Bergman had an infamous affair in 1949 with a director she later married. Who was he?

A Ingmar Bergman
B Roberto Rossellini
C David O. Selznick

4 Which of these parts of the United Kingdom is not a part of Britain?

A Northern Ireland
B Scotland
C Wales

5 What did Galahad, Perceval, Tristan and Mordred all have in common?

A All were in the 1977 Boat Race winning team
B All were Knights of the Round Table
C All were ancient Welsh castles

6 What is a greenstick fracture?

A A softwood branch split off a tree
B A freshly broken mineral or rock
C An incomplete fracture in a child's bone

7 What arrived in Britain in 1347?

A Gunpowder-fired artillery
B The Black Death
C Trial by jury

8 What is the world's longest rail journey?

A Perth to Sydney
B Halifax to Vancouver
C Moscow to Vladivostok

9 What is the fastest land mammal over a short distance?

A Cheetah
B Pronghorn antelope
C White-tailed gnu

10 What film earned John Wayne his only Oscar?

A *The Quiet Man*
B *The Searchers*
C *True Grit*

11 What event in 1447 was said by some to pave the way for the Reformation?

A The discovery of printing
B Publication of the first vernacular Bible
C Birth of Martin Luther

12 What was the sequel to *Porridge*?

A *On The Outside*
B *Going Straight*
C *Now What?*

A
13

1 B
2 B
3 A
4 B
5 C
6 B
7 C
8 B
9 A
10 B
11 A
12 C

33

1 What Norse warriors worked themselves into a bloodthirsty frenzy before battle?

 A Berserkers
 B Furies
 C Nütters

2 Who is credited with devising the first waterproof fabric?

 A Charles Macintosh
 B James Watt
 C Richard Arkwright

3 How many points would a snooker player score for potting a red then a brown ball?

 A 3
 B 4
 C 5

4 What stage show gave Jason Donovan his 1991 hit, *Any Dream Will Do*?

 A *Cats*
 B *Les Miserables*
 C *Joseph & The Amazing Technicolor Dreamcoat*

5 What is a banderole?

 A A pennant
 B A bandstand
 C A type of sash

6 What was James Fenimore Cooper's character Uncas The Last Of?

 A The Red-Hot Lovers
 B His Tribe
 C The Mohicans

7 What group of Greek islands is Corfu in?

    A Ionian Islands
    B Cyclades
    C Dodecanese

8 What comedy writer and actor sang the theme song for *One Foot In The Grave*?

    A Rowan Atkinson
    B Neil Innes
    C Eric Idle

9 Who is the Greek god of sleep and dreams?

    A Morpheus
    B Anaestheseus
    C Comatus

10 What country won the first Eurovision Song Contest?

    A France
    B Switzerland
    C Norway

11 What film ends with the line, 'He ran them off their feet'?

    A *Chariots of Fire*
    B *Three Days of the Condor*
    C *The Running Man*

12 What is the only place in the world where there is no cold virus?

    A Antarctica
    B The Amazon Rainforest
    C The Sahara Desert

A 14

1	B
2	C
3	B
4	A
5	B
6	C
7	B
8	C
9	A
10	C
11	A
12	B

35

1 Porthos and Aramis were two of the Three Musketeers; who was the third?

A D'Artagnan
B Athos
C Richelieu

2 Russian-born Igor Sikorsky designed the first successful what?

A Motorbike
B Helicopter
C Machine gun

3 In what war did the Light Brigade charge?

A Boer War
B Crimean War
C Indian Mutiny

4 What would you do with an ocarina?

A Eat it
B Play it
C Frame it

5 Complete George Bush's 1991 comment: 'We need a nation closer to the Waltons than to...'?

A The Corleones
B The Simpsons
C The Clintons

6 What is the longest bone in the human body?

A Femur (hip to knee)
B Tibia (knee to ankle)
C Sternum (breastbone)

7 Where is Nelson's flagship, The Victory, to be seen?

    A Southampton
    B Portsmouth
    C London

8 Orchestral Manoeuvres in the Dark had a 1980 hit with *Enola Gay*; what was the song about?

    A The sterility of modern architecture
    B The lead singer's unhappy personal relationship
    C The plane that dropped the bomb on Hiroshima

9 What city has the Prado gallery?

    A Bologna
    B Madrid
    C Lisbon

10 Who played the patriotic musical American George M. Cohan in *Yankee Doodle Dandy*?

    A Mickey Rooney
    B Bing Crosby
    C James Cagney

11 What relation was the witch Morgan le Fay to King Arthur?

    A Illegitimate daughter
    B Half-sister
    C Birth mother

12 What county cricket side plays at the St Lawrence Ground?

    A Worcestershire
    B Durham
    C Kent

A 15

1	A
2	A
3	C
4	C
5	A
6	C
7	A
8	C
9	A
10	B
11	A
12	A

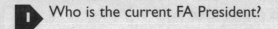

QUESTIONS 17

1 Who is the current FA President?

   A Duke of Kent
   B Duke of York
   C Duke of Edinburgh

2 What miraculous food was given to the Israelites wandering in the wilderness?

   A Figs
   B Carob
   C Manna

3 Whose daughters were Goneril, Regan and Cordelia?

   A King Arthur
   B Brian Boru, High King of Ireland
   C King Lear

4 What is a motte?

   A A moat around a castle
   B A mound a castle sits on
   C A coat of arms carved in stone on a castle

5 What musical does the football anthem *You'll Never Walk Alone* come from?

   A *Carousel*
   B *The Great Game*
   C *Escape to Victory*

6 What name is given to young pilchards?

   A Whitebait
   B Sardines
   C Anchovies

7 What 90s grunge band featured Krist Novoselic and Dave Grohl?

    A Smashing Pumpkins
    B Nirvana
    C Pearl Jam

8 What area was Jacob Epstein famous in?

    A Medicine
    B Music
    C Sculpture

9 What country has more bikes than any other?

    A India
    B China
    C Netherlands

10 What astrological sign comes after Cancer and before Virgo?

    A Gemini
    B Libra
    C Leo

11 In geometry, what is a reflex angle?

    A One that is more than 90° but less than 180
    B One that, when added to another, makes up 90°
    C One that is more than 180° but less than 360

12 Who sang the punk cult classic *White Man In Hammersmith Palais*?

    A The Damned
    B The Clash
    C The Sex Pistols

A 16

1	B
2	B
3	B
4	B
5	B
6	A
7	B
8	C
9	B
10	C
11	B
12	C

1 What is the notorious tidal current in the Lofoten Islands off northern Norway called?

A The Maelstrom
B The Gulf Stream
C The Hellespont

2 What is the disorder *Sydenham's chorea* often called?

A St Vitus's dance
B Lazy eye
C Hunchback

3 If you were in Amman, what country's capital would you be in?

A Thailand
B Jordan
C Central African Republic

4 In what film does Jack Nicholson announce his arrival with the declaration, 'Here's Johnny!'?

A *The Terror*
B *Little Shop of Horrors*
C *The Shining*

5 What opera was legally limited by its composer to be performed with all black actors?

A *Otello*
B *Porgy and Bess*
C *Street Scene*

6 What European country was ruled by King Zog until 1946?

A Romania
B Albania
C Montenegro

7 What Victorian literary scoundrel did George Macdonald Fraser make an anti-hero?

   A Bill Sykes
   B Flashman
   C Uriah Heep

8 Ultravox's atmospheric 1981 classic *Vienna* was kept from the number one spot by what song?

   A *Shaddap You Face* by Joe Dolce
   B *Imagine* by John Lennon
   C *Making Your Mind Up* by Bucks Fizz

9 What US president's previous jobs included that of male model?

   A Ronald Reagan
   B Gerald Ford
   C John F. Kennedy

10 In pottery terminology, what is a banker?

   A A workbench
   B A type of hard, white pottery
   C Something sure to sell well

11 What was the name of the Lone Ranger's horse?

   A Silver
   B Trigger
   C Tonto

12 What type of sherry is oloroso?

   A Very dry and pale
   B Medium
   C Dark and sweet

1	B
2	C
3	C
4	B
5	A
6	B
7	B
8	C
9	B
10	C
11	C
12	B

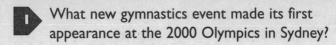
1 What new gymnastics event made its first appearance at the 2000 Olympics in Sydney?

   A Trampolining
   B Rope climbing
   C Club swinging

2 What was the name of the song that gave the Bloodhound Gang a UK hit in summer 2000?

   A *The Bad Touch*
   B *Discovery Channel*
   C *Nothin' But Mammals*

3 What was the Bounty's work in the South Seas before the mutiny?

   A Charting the seas
   B Collecting breadfruit
   C Trading with the islanders

4 What is the average life expectancy of a tortoise?

   A Over 80 years
   B Over 100 years
   C Over 150 years

5 What type of headdress was traditionally worn by triumphant Roman generals?

   A Their helmet
   B A silver crown
   C A wreath of laurel leaves

6 Who played the title role in the classic BBC drama, *I Claudius*?

   A John Hurt
   B Patrick Stewart
   C Derek Jacobi

7 According to the *Book of Genesis*, who first bought Joseph as a slave in Egypt?

A Pharaoh
B Potiphar
C A coat manufacturer

8 Which of these Dubliners did not win the Nobel Prize for Literature?

A Samuel Beckett
B James Joyce
C George Bernard Shaw

9 Where might you have expected to find a shovel hat?

A Driving machinery at a pit-head
B Sitting on a clergyman's head
C Taking part in an archaeological dig

10 What was the name of Bing Crosby's boat in *High Society*?

A *High Society*
B *The True Love*
C *Samantha*

11 In theatrical terms, what were groundlings?

A Those standing in the cheap section of a theatre
B Those who helped backstage in productions
C Boys who took women's roles in productions

12 Which of Britain's intelligence services is known as the Secret Intelligence Service?

A MI4
B MI5
C MI6

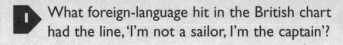
1 What foreign-language hit in the British chart had the line, 'I'm not a sailor, I'm the captain'?

  A La Bamba
  B La Mer
  C La Vie En Rose

2 What TV show gave Danny de Vito his big break?

  A *Cheers*
  B *Taxi*
  C *Roseanne*

3 What film saw Jeremy Brett serenade Audrey Hepburn from the street outside her house?

  A *Breakfast At Tiffany's*
  B *Roman Holiday*
  C *My Fair Lady*

4 What is Charles Goodyear credited with inventing in 1839?

  A Moulds for carriage wheels
  B Vulcanised rubber
  C The pneumatic tyre

5 Where is the Giant's Causeway?

  A The Hebrides
  B The west coast of Scotland
  C The north coast of Ireland

6 Who was the first person to reach the South Pole?

  A Roald Amundsen
  B Captain Scott
  C Ernest Shackleton

7 What African country did Ian Smith once rule?

    A Rhodesia
    B Zimbabwe
    C South Africa

8 Cocaine was once an ingredient of what popular drink?

    A Lucozade
    B Ovaltine
    C Coca-Cola

9 What media mogul's personal plane, the Spruce Goose, had the largest wingspan in the world?

    A Ted Turner
    B William Randolph Hearst
    C Howard Hughes

10 According to George Bernard Shaw's play, what was John Bull's Other Island?

    A The United States
    B Australia
    C Ireland

11 What is dried in an oast?

    A Oats
    B Hops
    C Wheat

12 In what sport is the Thomas Cup a prize?

    A Downhill skiing
    B Badminton
    C Dinghy sailing

A 19

1 A
2 A
3 B
4 A
5 C
6 C
7 B
8 B
9 B
10 B
11 A
12 C

45

1 If you had a hogshead of wine, how much wine would you have?

    A 24 gallons
    B 63 gallons
    C 144 gallons

2 What 60s cult TV show was devised and introduced by Rod Serling?

    A *The Monkees*
    B *Star Trek*
    C *The Twilight Zone*

3 What was Huey Lewis and the News theme song for the film classic *Back To The Future*?

    A *The Power of Love*
    B *Do You Believe In Love?*
    C *Hip To Be Square*

4 If it rains on St Swithin's Day, 15th July, how many days' rain does the old rhyme say will follow?

    A 20
    B 40
    C 50

5 What name is given to the five lines that music is written on?

    A Bars
    B Scale
    C Staff

6 Whose stated intention was it to blow the Scots back to Scotland?

    A Margaret Thatcher
    B Samuel Johnson
    C The Gunpowder plotters

7 Competitive swimming has four events: breaststroke, backstroke, butterfly… and what?

   A Front crawl
   B Freestyle
   C Forward stroke

8 Who was the last Prime Minister of Northern Ireland?

   A David Trimble
   B Brian Faulkner
   C James Chichester-Clark

9 What year did food rationing end in Britain?

   A 1945
   B 1954
   C 1949

10 Who is the first character Dorothy meets on the road to Oz?

   A The Tin Man
   B The Cowardly Lion
   C The Scarecrow

11 The fictional 17th-century Spanish romantic Don Quixote became the star of what musical?

   A *Lost In The Stars*
   B *Man Of La Mancha*
   C *Mr Wonderful*

12 What, according to Christ, was the greatest of the three main virtues?

   A Love
   B Faith
   C Hope

A
20

1 A
2 B
3 C
4 B
5 C
6 A
7 A
8 C
9 C
10 C
11 B
12 B

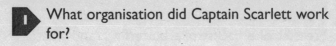
1 What organisation did Captain Scarlett work for?

   A Rainbow
   B Spectrum
   C Prism

2 What Italian guerrilla fighter had a biscuit named after him?

   A Bourbon
   B Garibaldi
   C Savoiardi

3 Which of the following countries has never had an Irish-born president or prime minister?

   A New Zealand
   B Israel
   C USA

4 What drug was initially derived from willow-tree bark?

   A Penicillin
   B Aspirin
   C Opium

5 What is carpology the study of?

   A Some types of fish
   B Fruit and seeds
   C Textiles

6 What US state are the Catskill Mountains in?

   A New York
   B Pennsylvania
   C Connecticut

7 Which of the following TV series has never become a motion picture?

    A *Dad's Army*
    B *On The Buses*
    C *Are You Being Served?*

8 What was Marillion's biggest UK hit?

    A *Kayleigh*
    B *Romeo and Juliet*
    C *Lavender*

9 What Irish actor has been Oscar-nominated seven times but has never won?

    A Kenneth Branagh
    B Peter O'Toole
    C Liam Neeson

10 Who was the first Archbishop of Canterbury?

    A St Alban
    B St Augustine
    C St Aidan

11 What county cricket club's colours are dark green and scarlet?

    A Leicestershire
    B Middlesex
    C Glamorgan

12 What platform at King's Cross Station does the Hogwarts Express leave from?

    A $8^{1/2}$
    B $9^{1/4}$
    C $9^{3/4}$

1 B
2 C
3 A
4 B
5 C
6 C
7 B
8 B
9 B
10 C
11 B
12 A

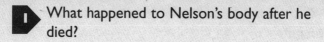

1 What happened to Nelson's body after he died?

A He was buried at sea
B He was pickled in brandy and shipped home
C He was embalmed and shipped home

2 Green and orange are two of the secondary colours. What is the third?

A White
B Brown
C Purple

3 How was the Sword of Damocles suspended?

A By a chain of gold
B By a single hair
C From an eagle's claw

4 What is the adult leader of a Brownie pack called?

A Barn Owl
B Brown Owl
C Tawny Owl

5 What was the name of Mickey Mouse's dog?

A Pluto
B Goofy
C Dumbo

6 Who won the Women's Football World Cup in 2003?

A Australia
B Germany
C China

7 What US president was elected to office four times?

    A Abraham Lincoln
    B Richard Nixon
    C Franklin D. Roosevelt

8 Complete the quotation: 'The way to a man's heart is through his ...'

    A Chest
    B Stomach
    C Vanity

9 What cathedral has the tallest spire in England?

    A Salisbury
    B Gloucester
    C Westminster

10 In *The Wind in the Willows*, what reckless driver was imprisoned?

    A Toad
    B Rat
    C Mole

11 Where is the CNN organisation based?

    A New York
    B Atlanta
    C Washington, DC

12 Who was thought to have washed his hands of Christ's final fate?

    A King Herod
    B Pontius Pilate
    C Caiaphas, the High Priest

1	B
2	B
3	C
4	B
5	B
6	A
7	C
8	A
9	B
10	B
11	A
12	C

1 What modern British political party was founded by a man who also founded his own church?

    A Natural Law Party
    B Democratic Unionist Party
    C Monster Raving Loony Party

2 Who were the couple featured in the Kinks' 1967 hit *Waterloo Sunset*?

    A Terry and Julie
    B Terry and Susie
    C Terry and June

3 Whose nemesis is Elmer Fudd?

    A Daffy Duck
    B Bugs Bunny
    C Porky Pig

4 What name is given to a narrow strip of land that bridges two larger land areas?

    A Peninsula
    B Isthmus
    C Atoll

5 Who was called Britain's once and future king?

    A Harold
    B Alfred
    C Arthur

6 What company made the world's first-ever personal computer?

    A IBM
    B Microsoft
    C Apple

7 'Working with her was like being hit over the head with a Valentine's card'. Who was being described?

- **A** Doris Day
- **B** Sandra Dee
- **C** Julie Andrews

8 What Olympic sport prohibits the wearing of a beard?

- **A** Weightlifting
- **B** Boxing
- **C** Synchronised swimming

9 In the children's song, what do *The Wheels On The Bus* do?

- **A** Roll all over town
- **B** Go round and round
- **C** Stop and start

10 Which of these was not one of Snow White's dwarves in the Disney animated feature film?

- **A** Cheerful
- **B** Grumpy
- **C** Sleepy

11 What is Hamas?

- **A** A Middle-Eastern chickpea dish
- **B** A Turkish holiday resort
- **C** An anti-Israeli terror group

12 What is the capital of the Italian region of Lazio?

- **A** Rome
- **B** Naples
- **C** Bologna

A
23

1 **B**
2 **C**
3 **B**
4 **B**
5 **A**
6 **B**
7 **C**
8 **B**
9 **A**
10 **A**
11 **B**
12 **B**

1 Who devised a new set of rules to clean up boxing in 1869?

   A Prince Albert
   B The Marquis of Queensberry
   C Benjamin Disraeli

2 Roughly how long ago was the wheel invented?

   A 5500 BC
   B 4500 BC
   C 3500 BC

3 Which city is said to have been founded by Romulus and Remus?

   A Venice
   B Rome
   C Florence

4 Where would you find the Royal and Ancient Club?

   A St Andrews
   B Troon
   C Muirfield

5 What British store was the first to offer its customers self-service?

   A Marks & Spencer
   B Tesco
   C Sainsbury's

6 What school do Mrs Krabappel and Principal Skinner teach in?

   A Grange Hill
   B Springfield Elementary
   C Sunnydale High

7 What is the final book in *The Lord of the Rings* trilogy?

A The Return Of The Ring
B The Return Of The King
C The Return Of The Thing

8 In the classic comedy show *Bewitched*, what was the name of Samantha's mother?

A Tabitha
B Endora
C Clara

9 What ex-Beatle had a top 10 hit in 1971 with *Bangla Desh*?

A John Lennon
B George Harrison
C Ringo Starr

10 Where did the name of chart toppers T'Pau come from?

A A Vulcan official in Star Trek
B A Japanese word for 'peace'
C The band members' initials

11 What is the oldest of the major religions still practised today?

A Hinduism
B Judaism
C Buddhism

12 Where is a fish's dorsal fin?

A It's the fish's tail
B Below the fish's body
C On top of the fish's body

1 B
2 A
3 B
4 B
5 C
6 C
7 C
8 B
9 B
10 A
11 C
12 A

1 In *The Hitch-Hiker's Guide To The Galaxy*, what did a babel fish allow Arthur Dent to do?

  A Eat
  B Understand other languages
  C Escape from his captors

2 What sport, apart from badminton, uses a shuttlecock?

  A Lacrosse
  B Real tennis
  C Battledore

3 What politician was called 'the Uncrowned King of Ireland'?

  A Michael Collins
  B Charles Stewart Parnell
  C Ian Paisley

4 What is Britain's biggest railway station?

  A Waterloo
  B King's Cross
  C Paddington

5 Who played Jake Blues' psychopathic love interest in the cult comedy *The Blues Brothers*?

  A Twiggy
  B Aretha Franklin
  C Carrie Fisher

6 What British organisation is the oldest scientific society in the world?

  A The Royal Society
  B The Royal Society of Science
  C The Society of Scientists

7 When was the first Thanksgiving in America?

    A 1621
    B 1776
    C 1812

8 Jimmy Pursey was lead singer with what 70s British stomp-rock band?

    A Slade
    B Status Quo
    C Sham 69

9 If you were in the city of Cheyenne, what American state would you be in?

    A Delaware
    B Oregon
    C Wyoming

10 Gingivitis is the name given to what?

    A Excess stomach acid
    B Gum inflammation
    C Flaking fingernails

11 What island did Father Ted have his parish on?

    A Rugged Island
    B Craggy Island
    C Rocky Island

12 What is the near-side of a car nearest to?

    A The pavement
    B The middle of the road
    C The traffic in front

1	B
2	C
3	B
4	A
5	C
6	B
7	B
8	B
9	B
10	A
11	A
12	C

1 What is the name of the dog in *Tom & Jerry*?

   A Butch
   B Spike
   C Ripper

2 Where was Prince Philip born?

   A Greece
   B Scotland
   C Romania

3 Who was the chief of the Norse gods?

   A Thor
   B Odin
   C Balder

4 What Shakespeare play had the subtitle *The Moor of Venice*?

   A *Coriolanus*
   B *Othello*
   C *King Lear*

5 Which military leader rode a horse called Bucephalus?

   A Napoleon
   B Alexander the Great
   C Duke of Marlborough

6 What was the Australian natural feature Uluru formerly known as?

   A Ayers Rock
   B The Outback
   C The Great Barrier Reef

7 Along with George Michael, who made up Wham!?

    A Andrew Taylor
    B Andrew Ridgeley
    C Andrew Roberts

8 Pride, envy and wrath are three of the what?

    A Four Gifts of Satan
    B Seven Deadly Sins
    C Nine Temptations of the Saints

9 What Bronski Beat song came from an opera by George Gershwin?

    A *Cha Cha Heels*
    B *It Ain't Necessarily So*
    C *Why?*

10 What first is Thomas Cook credited with?

    A First to offer a UK-wide stagecoach seat sale
    B First to offer a foreign currency exchange
    C First to offer a travel agent's service

11 How many faces does a cube have?

    A 4
    B 6
    C 8

12 What country produces more films than any other every year?

    A France
    B USA
    C India

A
26

1	B
2	C
3	B
4	A
5	C
6	A
7	A
8	C
9	C
10	B
11	B
12	A

1 What is the name of Long John Silver's parrot in *Treasure Island*?

A Captain Flint
B Jim Lad
C Polly

2 When was the hidden city of Petra discovered by a westerner?

A 1812
B 1847
C 1859

3 In which direction do tornadoes normally spin in the southern hemisphere?

A Clockwise
B Anti-clockwise
C Either way

4 What American state's nickname is the Bay State?

A Washington
B Massachusetts
C Georgia

5 What would an Italian do with panettone?

A Use it in printing
B Eat it
C Use it as a musical notation

6 What king of Scots went on to unite the crowns of Scotland and England?

A James VI
B James V
C James IV

7 Complete the list of weapons used in Fencing competitions: foil, epée ... and what?

   A Cutlass
   B Sabre
   C Rapier

8 Who is Buffy the Vampire Slayer's vampire lover?

   A Xander
   B Angel
   C Spike

9 What part of killer Gary Gilmore's body did The Adverts sing about in 1977?

   A Hands
   B Mouth
   C Eyes

10 In the film *Cabaret*, what nightclub was the backdrop to much of the action?

   A Ein, Zwei, Drei
   B Roxy
   C The Kit-Kat Club

11 What is the most common mineral on Earth?

   A Iron pyrite
   B Feldspar
   C Quartz

12 In the Kenny Rogers song *Coward of the County*, what was the coward's name?

   A Billy
   B Tommy
   C Bobby

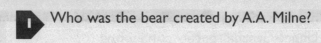

1 Who was the bear created by A.A. Milne?

A Rupert
B Paddington
C Winnie the Pooh

2 What was hung upside down in the Piazzale Loreto in Milan in 1945?

A Mussolini's body
B Mona Lisa
C The German flag

3 How many times, at the end of the 20th century, had Israel won the Eurovision Song Contest?

A 1
B 2
C 3

4 Where on a flag is the canton?

A The outside half, furthest from the flagpole
B The centre, where any emblems appear
C The upper quarter nearest the flagpole

5 What film was Berlin's 1986 hit *Take My Breath Away* the theme song for?

A Fatal Attraction
B Top Gun
C An Officer And A Gentleman

6 What type of product was *Take My Breath Away* used to advertise in a long-running campaign?

A Mouthrinse
B Cigarettes
C Cars

7 What modern-day province does the old district of Upper Canada roughly correspond to?

    A British Columbia
    B The Northwest Territories
    C Ontario

8 What is sauerkraut?

    A A German sausage
    B Shredded pickled cabbage
    C A mix of cabbage and carrot in mayonnaise

9 Who played the Cincinnati Kid?

    A Paul Newman
    B Steve McQueen
    C Alan Ladd

10 If the Pentateuch is the first five books of the Old Testament, what is the Heptateuch?

    A The next five
    B The next seven
    C The first seven

11 Who has made more test match appearances for England than any other cricketer?

    A Graham Gooch
    B David Gower
    C Colin Cowdrey

12 What colour would an acid turn litmus paper?

    A Blue
    B Red
    C Green

A
28

1	A
2	A
3	A
4	B
5	B
6	A
7	B
8	B
9	C
10	C
11	C
12	B

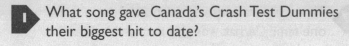

Q U E S T I O N S

30

1 What song gave Canada's Crash Test Dummies their biggest hit to date?

A *La La La*
B *Mmm Mmm Mmm Mmm*
C *Da Da Da*

2 To the nearest thousand, how many stars are visible to the naked eye?

A 17,000
B 9,000
C 2,000

3 What country is covered four-fifths by an ice sheet?

A Russia
B Finland
C Greenland

4 In Burns' poem of the same name, how does *Tam O' Shanter* escape from the pursuing witches?

A He hides in an empty grave
B He outruns them
C He crosses the river

5 What designer won Oscars for his costumes in *Gigi* and *My Fair Lady*?

A Christian Dior
B Cecil Beaton
C Hardy Amies

6 How wide is the hoop in basketball?

A 18 inches
B 24 inches
C 28 inches

7 Three generations of Indian PMs came from one family. What was the patriarch's name?

    A Gandhi
    B Nehru
    C Jinnah

8 What song is second to Frankie Laine's *I Believe* in length of time at number 1 in the UK?

    A *I Do It For You* by Bryan Adams
    B *Bohemian Rhapsody* by Queen
    C *Love Is All Around* by Wet Wet Wet

9 What was the island of Tasmania formerly known as?

    A Botany Bay
    B Van Diemen's Land
    C Cook's County

10 In the film *Time Bandits*, what was stolen from the Supreme Being?

    A A clock that let you travel freely through time
    B A map showing the Universe's time holes
    C The most precious object in the Universe

11 On the cover of the Beatles' *Abbey Road* album, who is wearing a white suit?

    A John Lennon
    B Ringo Starr
    C Paul McCartney

12 What was the name of the oil-rich family in *The Beverly Hillbillies*?

    A The Clintons
    B The Clantons
    C The Clampetts

1	C
2	A
3	C
4	C
5	B
6	C
7	C
8	B
9	B
10	C
11	A
12	B

1 When was sex testing introduced for athletes?

    A 1968
    B 1972
    C 1976

2 All dogs scratch at the same rate; what is it?

    A 3 times a second
    B 4 times a second
    C 5 times a second

3 Who was the leader of England's original New Model Army?

    A Oliver Cromwell
    B Charles I
    C Prince Rupert

4 What band was *Lifted* in 1995 and again in 1996?

    A Lighthouse Family
    B Lightning Seeds
    C Crowded House

5 What wartime classic movie did Noel Coward write, direct, compose the music and star in?

    A *In Which We Serve*
    B *Reach For The Sky*
    C *They Were Expendable*

6 Who was the first woman boss of MI5?

    A Stella Remmington
    B Stella Rimington
    C Stella Richardson

7 What was Jonathan Swift's satirical solution for childhood poverty and hunger in Ireland?

   A Poor children to be adopted by the rich
   B Poor children to be fattened & eaten by the rich
   C Poor children to be shipped to England

8 Who wrote the words to the song *My Way*?

   A Frank Sinatra
   B Paul Anka
   C Neil Sedaka

9 In Greek mythology, what fate befell Icarus?

   A He flew too near the sun on wax wings
   B He was eaten by the Minotaur
   C He was turned into a flower by the gods

10 What traditional British figure is mentioned in the 14th-century poem Piers Plowman?

   A Herne the Hunter
   B King Arthur
   C Robin Hood

11 What flavour is mulligatawny soup?

   A Curry flavoured
   B Fish flavoured
   C Tropical fruit flavoured

12 What is the name of the timid cartoon dog owned by Eustace and Muriel?

   A Coward
   B Custard
   C Courage

A
30

1 B
2 B
3 C
4 C
5 B
6 A
7 B
8 A
9 B
10 B
11 A
12 C

1 What river did Julius Caesar cross in 49 BC to challenge the authority of Rome's senators?

    A The Tiber
    B The Po
    C The Rubicon

2 What was the name of Bill Sykes' dog in *Oliver Twist*?

    A Bullseye
    B Bullhorn
    C Bullbar

3 The Beatles were the first British group to top the US singles chart; who were the second?

    A The Hollies
    B The Animals
    C The Rolling Stones

4 What are members of the Society of Friends better known as?

    A Plymouth Brethren
    B Quakers
    C Amish

5 In prehistoric times, what would you have expected to find in a barrow?

    A Buried bodies
    B Grain
    C Cave paintings of animals

6 What Scottish football team plays at New Broomfield?

    A Hearts
    B St Johnstone
    C Airdrie United

7 What cult 60s show featured TV's first interracial kiss?

    A *Star Trek*
    B *The Twilight Zone*
    C *The Man From U.N.C.L.E.*

8 How many flowering plants grow in Antarctica?

    A None
    B 2
    C 47

9 In which year did *Kramer v Kramer*, starring Dustin Hoffman and Meryl Streep, win the best film Oscar?

    A 1975
    B 1977
    C 1979

10 Which of these countries is NOT in the EU?

    A Slovakia
    B Slovenia
    C Bulgaria

11 What do the movies *The Terminator*, *Aliens* and *Titanic* have in common?

    A Someone called Di Caprio worked on each
    B All three were directed by the same person
    C A cat dies at the start of each one

12 Who was the American winner of the 1973 Nobel Peace Prize?

    A Richard Nixon
    B Gerald Ford
    C Henry Kissinger

A
31

1 A
2 C
3 A
4 A
5 A
6 B
7 B
8 B
9 A
10 C
11 A
12 C

69

1 In what century did Dick Whittington first become mayor of London?

    A 14th
    B 16th
    C 18th

2 How many points does a try earn in Rugby League?

    A 5
    B 3
    C 4

3 What band had a 1983 hit with *The Love Cats*?

    A Stray Cats
    B The Cure
    C Blondie

4 What would you expect to find in the libretto of an opera?

    A The music
    B The words
    C The directions to the orchestra

5 Who won the 1836 battle at The Alamo, Texas?

    A The Americans
    B The Mexicans
    C The Native American Indians

6 What film saw two characters forced to hide in drag after seeing the St Valentine's Day Massacre?

    A *The Untouchables*
    B *Once Upon A Time In America*
    C *Some Like It Hot*

7 What element does Kr represent on the Periodic Table?

    A Krypton
    B Curium
    C Potassium

8 In the language of flowers, what does the herb rosemary represent?

    A Falsehood
    B Remembrance
    C True love

9 What story saw Sherlock Holmes's first appearance?

    A *The Sign Of Four*
    B *The Hound of The Baskervilles*
    C *A Study In Scarlet*

10 In the 1980s TV version of Sherlock Holmes, two actors played Watson. Who were they?

    A Jeremy Brett & David Burke
    B David Burke & Edward Hardwicke
    C Edward Hardwicke & Jeremy Brett

11 The Japanese movie *The Seven Samurai* was remade as what?

    A Seven Brides for Seven Brothers
    B The Magnificent Seven
    C The Seventh Cross

12 Who was first to be buried in Westminster Abbey's Poets' Corner?

    A Geoffrey Chaucer
    B William Shakespeare
    C Ben Jonson

1	C
2	A
3	B
4	B
5	A
6	C
7	A
8	B
9	C
10	C
11	B
12	C

1 How many sonnets did Shakespeare publish?

A 69
B 102
C 154

2 In what century did the Renaissance begin in Italy?

A 14th century
B 15th century
C 16th century

3 What was the name of the dog in the children's TV series *The Herbs*?

A Dill
B Parsley
C Basil

4 What saint would pilgrims visiting Walsingham be honouring?

A St Thomas à Becket
B Edward the Confessor
C Our Lady

5 If someone is peregrinating, what are they doing?

A Swooping down on something
B Travelling from place to place
C Complaining about something

6 What family did Peter Pan visit?

A The Dearing Family
B The Darling Family
C The Downing Family

7 One of the 15th-century Princes in the Tower was Richard, Duke of York; who was the other?

A Edward, Prince of Wales
B Edward V
C Edward, Duke of Clarence

8 What country did badminton's ancestor game, poona, come from?

A Sri Lanka
B India
C China

9 Which of the 'Road' films, starring Crosby, Hope and Lamour, was first to be made?

A *Road to Singapore*
B *Road to Hong Kong*
C *Road to Utopia*

10 What was the abbreviated name of the old English county of Shropshire?

A Shron
B Shrops
C Salop

11 How much was a guinea worth?

A 5 shillings
B 12 shillings
C 21 shillings

12 What successful cabaret star had a 1968 hit with the unlikely title *Les Bicyclettes De Belsize*?

A Val Doonican
B Engelbert Humperdinck
C Andy Williams

1	A
2	C
3	B
4	B
5	B
6	C
7	A
8	B
9	C
10	B
11	B
12	A

73

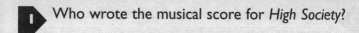

QUESTIONS 35

I Who wrote the musical score for *High Society*?

    A Cole Porter
    B Irving Berlin
    C George Gershwin

2 What song, by the Four Seasons and Divine, has the line, 'No woman's worth crawling on the earth'?

    A *Big Girls Don't Cry*
    B *Walk Like A Man*
    C *You Think You're A Man*

3 What British government official traditionally sat on the woolsack?

    A Minister for Agriculture
    B Lord Chancellor
    C Speaker of the House of Commons

4 What was the relationship between Princess Leia and Luke Skywalker in *Star Wars*?

    A They were lovers
    B They were cousins
    C They were brother and sister

5 What disorders does an endocrinologist treat?

    A Tumours
    B Hormone gland disorders
    C Joint disorders

6 How many players are there in a Canadian football team?

    A 11
    B 12
    C 13

7 The death of Laura Palmer was the central event for what cult 90s drama?

A *Northern Exposure*
B *Twin Peaks*
C *American Gothic*

8 What name is Robert Zimmerman better known by?

A Bob Seger
B Bob Hope
C Bob Dylan

9 What is Machu Picchu?

A A city of the Incas
B A type of coffee
C A Hindu god

10 On the eighth day of Christmas, what did my true love send to me?

A Eight drummers drumming
B Eight maids a-milking
C Eight ladies dancing

11 What sparked the Peasants' Revolt of 1381?

A A poll tax
B Compulsory Military Service
C Cancelling of Christmas holidays

12 What does the religious season of Lent commemorate?

A The exile of Jesus and his parents in Egypt
B The wanderings of the Israelites in the desert
C The time Christ spent fasting in the wilderness

1	**C**
2	**A**
3	**A**
4	**C**
5	**B**
6	**B**
7	**B**
8	**B**
9	**A**
10	**C**
11	**C**
12	**B**

1 Where did Thunderbird 4 spend its time?

   A In the air
   B Orbiting the earth
   C Underwater

2 What stone or substance did alchemists think would turn base metals into gold?

   A Warestone
   B Philosopher's stone
   C Runestone

3 What Scottish council area has Lerwick as its administrative town?

   A Ross and Cromarty
   B Orkney
   C Shetland

4 What 'first' was achieved by the Al Jolson film, *The Jazz Singer*?

   A First film where a white man pretended to be black
   B First musical film
   C First talking motion picture

5 Which of Henry VIII's wives was the mother of Edward VI?

   A Jane Seymour
   B Catherine Parr
   C Catherine Howard

6 What reformer wrote *The Rights Of Man* in support of the French Revolution?

   A Edmund Burke
   B Thomas Paine
   C Percy Bysshe Shelley

7 What was the only Jamiroquai song to enter the UK chart at number 1?

    A *Deeper Underground*
    B *Alright*
    C *Canned Heat*

8 In *Little Women*, three of the March sisters are Meg, Beth and Amy; who is the fourth?

    A Jo
    B Edith
    C Louisa

9 Who won the first Footballer of the Year award, in 1948?

    A Stanley Matthews
    B Joe Mercer
    C Billy Wright

10 What body parts had Lord Nelson lost by the start of the Battle of Trafalgar?

    A A leg and an eye
    B An arm and a leg
    C An arm and an eye

11 What city was the Moors' capital in Spain for over 150 years?

    A Seville
    B Malaga
    C Granada

12 What do blewit, parasol and fly agaric have in common?

    A They are types of butterfly
    B They are types of mushroom
    C They are types of wildflower

A
35

1 A
2 B
3 B
4 C
5 B
6 B
7 B
8 C
9 A
10 B
11 A
12 C

1 In the children's rhyme *Oranges and Lemons*, what do the bells of Old Bailey say?

    A When will that be?
    B You owe me five farthings
    C When will you pay me?

2 What prehistoric period saw the end of the dinosaurs?

    A Jurassic
    B Cretaceous
    C Triassic

3 Who directed the 1996 film *Michael Collins*?

    A Liam Neeson
    B Neil Jordan
    C Pierce Brosnan

4 Who was the first Englishman to win the British Formula 1 Grand Prix?

    A Graham Hill
    B Jim Clark
    C Stirling Moss

5 What is the purpose of a keel on an ocean-going vessel?

    A It prevents the vessel from being blown sideways
    B It warns of shallow water
    C It helps to fend off sharks

6 What country used to be called Burma?

    A Myanmar
    B Thailand
    C Sri Lanka

7 What religious group declared, "Tis the gift to be simple, 'Tis the gift to be free'?

   A Quakers
   B Shakers
   C Levellers

8 What TV programme featured the characters Mrs Goggins and Miss Hubbard?

   A *The Mr Men*
   B *Postman Pat*
   C *The Two Ronnies*

9 According to the Jan & Dean 1963 surf classic, where were there 'Two girls for every boy'?

   A Palisades Park
   B Santa Monica
   C Surf City

10 How much was a farthing worth?

   A A quarter penny
   B Half a penny
   C Two pennies

11 John Milton wrote *Paradise Lost*; who wrote *Paradise Regained*?

   A John Milton
   B Percy Bysshe Shelley
   C William Blake

12 Charlie Chaplin's father-in-law was a Nobel Prize-winning writer. Who was he?

   A George Bernard Shaw
   B Eugene O'Neill
   C W.B. Yeats

A
36

1	C
2	B
3	C
4	C
5	A
6	B
7	A
8	A
9	A
10	C
11	C
12	B

1 What Eurovision Song Contest winner ran for the presidency of her native country in 1997?

   A Agnetha Faltskog of Abba
   B Dana
   C Dana International

2 What cartoonist created the Doonesbury strip?

   A Scott Adams
   B Charles Schultz
   C Garry Trudeau

3 On the electromagnetic spectrum, what has the shortest wavelength?

   A Microwaves
   B Radio and TV waves
   C Gamma rays

4 What did the Rosetta Stone provide the key to?

   A Translation of ancient Egyptian texts
   B Ancient Egyptians' knowledge of the stars
   C The whereabouts of Tutankhamun's tomb

5 What colour is Bobby Shaftoe's hair?

   A Yellow
   B Dark brown
   C Jet black

6 What film had its name changed to Tuesday the 13th in Latin America?

   A Friday the 13th
   B Thelma and Louise
   C Pat Garrett and Billy the Kid

7 The name Utopia comes from the Greek language. What does it mean?

  A Heavenly place
  B No place
  C Ideal place

8 Who has scored most goals for England?

  A Bobby Charlton
  B Gary Lineker
  C Jimmy Greaves

9 What sea lies off Italy's east coast?

  A Ionian
  B Adriatic
  C Ligurian

10 What was the name of Starsky and Hutch's boss?

  A Captain Huggy
  B Captain Dobey
  C Captain Walsh

11 What does Maundy Money, given out at Westminster Abbey in Holy Week, commemorate?

  A Christ washing his disciples' feet at the Last Supper
  B Christ's instruction to give all one has to the poor
  C Christ evicting money changers from the Temple

12 Who was executed on Elizabeth I's orders at Fotheringhay Castle?

  A Walter Raleigh
  B Francis Drake
  C Mary, Queen of Scots

1	C
2	B
3	B
4	C
5	A
6	A
7	B
8	B
9	C
10	A
11	A
12	B

1 How many players are there on a baseball team?

    A 9
    B 6
    C 8

2 Which of the Knights of the Round Table was called 'the Bold'?

    A Lancelot
    B Gawain
    C Bedivere

3 What playing card is known as the devil's four-poster bed?

    A Four of spades
    B Ace of spades
    C Four of clubs

4 How many black keys are there on a normal-sized piano?

    A 28
    B 32
    C 35

5 What uplifting invention was created by Elisha Otis?

    A The bra
    B The passenger lift
    C The jet engine

6 Who created the detective Inspector Maigret?

    A Agatha Christie
    B Georges Simenon
    C Colin Dexter

7 What singer/songwriter was *Killing Me Softly With His Song* written about?

    A Paul Simon
    B Don McLean
    C James Taylor

8 What cartoon character did Robin Williams play in a 1980 movie?

    A Dick Tracy
    B Batman
    C Popeye

9 How many copies of Magna Carta still exist today?

    A None
    B 1
    C 4

10 Where would you expect to find a Galvayne's groove?

    A On a compact disc
    B In a horse's tooth
    C In an Arthurian legend

11 What state did the USA buy from Spain in 1819?

    A California
    B Florida
    C New Mexico

12 What 60s western series, set in Arizona & New Mexico, featured the Cannon and Montoya families?

    A *Bonanza*
    B *The Big Valley*
    C *The High Chaparral*

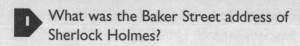

QUESTIONS 40

1 What was the Baker Street address of Sherlock Holmes?

    A 220B
    B 221B
    C 222B

2 What makes up Olympic Games Equestrian Events along with Dressage and Showjumping?

    A Cross-country
    B Three-day Event
    C Endurance

3 What American president suffered from polio as an adult?

    A Franklin D. Roosevelt
    B Harry Truman
    C Woodrow Wilson

4 How long was the important medieval English weapon, the longbow?

    A 5 feet
    B 6 feet
    C 7 feet

5 What do Dan Aykroyd, Bill Murray, John Belushi and Eddie Murphy have in common?

    A They were all in *The Blues Brothers*
    B They are all Canadian
    C They all got their break on *Saturday Night Live*

6 Matthew, Mark and John were three of the four evangelist Gospel authors; who was the fourth?

    A Andrew
    B Luke
    C Paul

7 What states did the Pony Express mail service operate between?

    A New York and California
    B Louisiana and California
    C Missouri and California

8 In what eastern American city would you find Logan Airport?

    A Boston
    B Baltimore
    C Bangor

9 What film and TV actor is also a successful rap star?

    A Vanilla Ice
    B Will Smith
    C Samuel L. Jackson

10 What does it mean when Lloyd's Lutine Bell is rung one time?

    A Good news
    B Bad news
    C No news

11 What movie ends with the line, 'Louis, I think this is the beginning of a beautiful friendship'?

    A *Casablanca*
    B *High Society*
    C *Young Frankenstein*

12 What bird has the widest wingspan in the world, at a width in excess of 11 feet 6 in (3.5m)?

    A Siberian crane
    B Great black-backed gull
    C Wandering albatross

1 Who said in 1970, justifying the US intervention in Cambodia, 'We are all the President's men'?

A G. Gordon Liddy
B Henry Kissinger
C Gerald Ford

2 Who played investigative reporter Bob Woodward in the 1976 film *All The President's Men*?

A Robert Redford
B Dustin Hoffman
C Jason Robards

3 What are Formosa Oolong, Orange Pekoe and Assam all types of?

A Decorative brickwork
B Exotic flower
C Tea

4 What pop and rock legend was born with the unpromising name Anna Mae Bullock?

A Whitney Houston
B Cher
C Tina Turner

5 What is the Zodiac symbol of two fishes called?

A Pisces
B Aries
C Aquarius

6 In the classic Mark Twain stories of *Tom Sawyer*, who is Tom's best friend?

A Uncle Remus
B Huckleberry Finn
C Jim the Slave

7 How do riders stop their bikes in Speedway?

    A Drag their feet on the ground
    B Apply their brakes
    C Run into specially padded walls

8 What is the most frequently transplanted body tissue?

    A Skin
    B Blood
    C Cornea

9 What 1950s film resurrected Frank Sinatra's career as it looked to be coming to a halt?

    A *Young at Heart*
    B *High Society*
    C *From Here to Eternity*

10 How was the Black Death spread?

    A By rats
    B By rat fleas
    C By rat faeces

11 How many miles is it from Land's End to John o' Groats?

    A 765
    B 876
    C 987

12 Fleegle, Bingo and Drooper are three of the Banana Splits. Who is the fourth?

    A Dorky
    B Korky
    C Snorky

1	B
2	B
3	A
4	B
5	C
6	B
7	C
8	A
9	B
10	A
11	A
12	C

1 What Dickens novel features a ruinous lawsuit between Jarndyce and Jarndyce?

A *Bleak House*
B *Great Expectations*
C *Hard Times*

2 What did Lee Strasberg teach in his New York studio?

A Method acting
B Expressionist painting
C Modernist sculpture

3 In what group did Mickey Dolenz play drums and Davy Jones sing?

A The Dave Clark Five
B The Monkees
C Dave Dee, Dozy, Beaky, Mick and Titch

4 When was a football league match first broadcast on radio in Britain?

A 1927
B 1933
C 1936

5 What is the length of the average term newborn baby?

A 20 inches
B 23 inches
C 25 inches

6 What proportion of the Sahara Desert is sand?

A Four-fifths
B Almost half
C One-fifth

7 What American president's New Deal rescued the Dustbowl States from poverty?

   A Theodore Roosevelt
   B Franklin D. Roosevelt
   C John F. Kennedy

8 D.H. Lawrence's *Lady Chatterley's Lover* was written in 1928; when was it published in full?

   A 1929
   B 1945
   C 1960

9 What female singer starred in the film *The Bodyguard* with Kevin Costner?

   A Madonna
   B Barbra Streisand
   C Whitney Houston

10 What Canadian band's only hit to date was *Echo Beach*?

   A Voggue
   B Martha and the Muffins
   C Men Without Hats

11 How many people make up a jury in Scotland?

   A 12
   B 13
   C 15

12 Strings, Woodwind and Brass are three sections of a symphony orchestra; what is the fourth?

   A Pianos
   B The conductor
   C Percussion

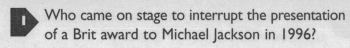

1 Who came on stage to interrupt the presentation of a Brit award to Michael Jackson in 1996?

- **A** Damon Albarn
- **B** Liam Gallagher
- **C** Jarvis Cocker

2 When is Herod's Slaughter of the Innocents after the birth of Jesus traditionally remembered?

- **A** 26th December
- **B** 1st January
- **C** 6th January

3 What classic western film did the story *The Tin Star* become?

- **A** *High Noon*
- **B** *Gunfight At The OK Corral*
- **C** *Shane*

4 What colour do judges wear with their black robes for criminal cases?

- **A** Blue
- **B** Lilac
- **C** Shocking pink

5 Whose secretary was Miss Moneypenny?

- **A** 007's
- **B** M's
- **C** Q's

6 What island's motto is 'Whichever way you throw me I will stand'?

- **A** The Falkland Islands
- **B** The Isle of Man
- **C** The Isle of Wight

7 What was Captain Thomas Blood pardoned by Charles II for?

   A Stealing the English crown jewels
   B Trying to kidnap the king
   C Raiding British ships on the Spanish Main

8 Up to the start of 2000, what was Neneh Cherry's only number 1 hit?

   A *Love Can Build A Bridge*
   B *7 Seconds*
   C *Buffalo Stance*

9 If a horse is measured at 18 hands, how high is it?

   A 4 feet 6 inches
   B 6 feet
   C 9 feet 9 inches

10 What famous crime writer has also written under the name Mary Westmacott?

   A Ruth Rendell
   B Patricia Cornwell
   C Agatha Christie

11 What cult show's slogan was 'I am not a number. I am a free man'?

   A *The Prisoner*
   B *The Fugitive*
   C *The Saint*

12 Who said, 'Je suis la France'?

   A Marie Antoinette
   B Napoleon
   C General Charles de Gaulle

1 A
2 A
3 B
4 A
5 A
6 C
7 B
8 C
9 C
10 B
11 C
12 C

1 What West Indian island was home to international cricketer Gary Sobers?

    A Barbados
    B Jamaica
    C Guyana

2 Roughly what is the Earth's circumference around the equator?

    A 31,026 miles
    B 15,807 miles
    C 24,902 miles

3 Who was Sooty's doggy sidekick?

    A Soo
    B Sweep
    C Brush

4 What rate is VAT currently charged at?

    A 12.5%
    B 17.5%
    C 20%

5 What Scottish holy island has been for centuries a burial place of kings and leaders?

    A Holy Island
    B Skye
    C Iona

6 Who led the Indian tribes at the Battle of the Little Bighorn?

    A Geronimo
    B Spotted Tail
    C Sitting Bull

7 Who first had a hit with *Lucy In The Sky With Diamonds*?

    A The Beatles
    B Elton John
    C David Bowie

8 What British writer is credited with creating the first full-length detective novels?

    A Charles Dickens
    B Arthur Conan Doyle
    C Wilkie Collins

9 From what London railway station would you leave if you were travelling to Manchester?

    A King's Cross
    B Euston
    C Paddington

10 The movie *Cry Freedom* told the story of what South African activist?

    A Nelson Mandela
    B Steve Biko
    C Oliver Tambo

11 The four Inns of Court are Middle Temple, Inner Temple, Gray's Inn … and what other?

    A Lincoln's Inn
    B Gray's Temple
    C Lincoln's Temple

12 On what bleak island was French Army officer Alfred Dreyfus falsely imprisoned for treason?

    A Devil's Island
    B St Helena
    C Elba

A
43

1	C
2	A
3	A
4	A
5	B
6	B
7	A
8	A
9	B
10	C
11	A
12	C

1 Which of the following has not recorded the theme song for a Bond movie?

A A-Ha
B Sheena Easton
C Aretha Franklin

2 Who was Hamlet's lover who drowned herself?

A Cordelia
B Ophelia
C Antonia

3 What is the Plimsoll line?

A The mark left by sandshoes on bare feet
B WWII defences on the Franco-German border
C The ship-side mark showing the safe loading limit

4 According to ancient Greek legend, what was at the centre of the Labyrinth on Crete?

A The Minotaur
B The Golden Fleece
C Medusa

5 What was Bruce Springsteen's first UK hit?

A *Born To Run*
B *Hungry Heart*
C *Dancing In The Dark*

6 What 1961 film won 10 Oscars?

A *The Guns of Navarone*
B *Breakfast at Tiffany's*
C *West Side Story*

7 What side was the first to follow a World Cup win with a European Championship win?

    A Italy
    B France
    C Netherlands

8 Who wrote *Auld Lang Syne*?

    A James VI of Scotland
    B William McGonagall
    C Robert Burns

9 How many digits do *The Simpsons* have on each hand?

    A 6
    B 5
    C 4

10 How long did the Hundred Years' War last between England and France?

    A 98 years
    B 102 years
    C 116 years

11 What musical featured the song *I'm Just A Girl Who Can't Say No*?

    A *Cabaret*
    B *Calamity Jane*
    C *Oklahoma!*

12 When were parking meters first introduced?

    A 1958
    B 1963
    C 1965

1	A
2	C
3	B
4	B
5	C
6	C
7	B
8	C
9	B
10	B
11	A
12	A

1 What was Sherlock Holmes' favourite vice?

  A Breaking and entering
  B Injecting cocaine
  C Frequenting gin palaces

2 In what sport did Graeme Obree make his name?

  A Archery
  B Swimming
  C Cycling

3 Who is actress Betty Joan Perske better known as?

  A Sigourney Weaver
  B Lauren Bacall
  C Kathleen Turner

4 What is the smallest planet in our solar system?

  A Mercury
  B Pluto
  C Uranus

5 According to the song, what mountains in Ireland sweep down to the sea?

  A The Wicklow Hills
  B MacGillycuddy's Reeks
  C The Mourne Mountains

6 What film's theme was the 1983 hit *Going Home*?

  A *Chariots of Fire*
  B *Local Hero*
  C *On Golden Pond*

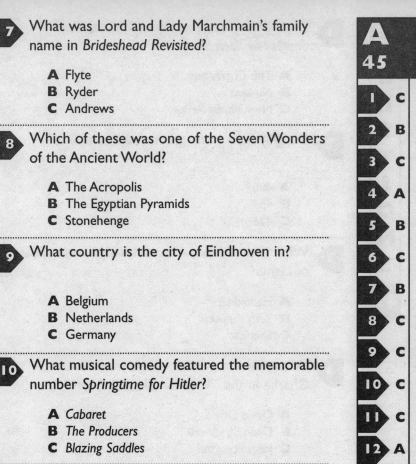

7 What was Lord and Lady Marchmain's family name in *Brideshead Revisited*?

    A Flyte
    B Ryder
    C Andrews

8 Which of these was one of the Seven Wonders of the Ancient World?

    A The Acropolis
    B The Egyptian Pyramids
    C Stonehenge

9 What country is the city of Eindhoven in?

    A Belgium
    B Netherlands
    C Germany

10 What musical comedy featured the memorable number *Springtime for Hitler*?

    A *Cabaret*
    B *The Producers*
    C *Blazing Saddles*

11 What hills separate Scotland and England?

    A The Cheviots
    B The Pennines
    C The Tweeds

12 What stopped Dick Whittington leaving London at Highgate and made him turn around again?

    A His cat persuaded him out of it
    B His horse threw a shoe
    C He heard the sound of the Bow bells

A
45

1 **C**
2 **B**
3 **C**
4 **A**
5 **B**
6 **C**
7 **B**
8 **C**
9 **C**
10 **C**
11 **C**
12 **A**

1 Who performed the seminal 90s anthem *Smells Like Teen Spirit?*

    A The Charlatans
    B Nirvana
    C New Model Army

2 Roughly how many grams are in a pound?

    A 400
    B 454
    C 426

3 What is the Hebrew name for the Jewish Feast of Lights?

    A Hanukkah
    B Yom Kippur
    C Shabbat

4 Who played the voice of the never-seen Charlie in the TV series *Charlie's Angels?*

    A David Doyle
    B Dean Stockwell
    C John Forsythe

5 What flavouring is used in the liqueur amaretto?

    A Almonds
    B Coffee
    C Lemons

6 What family feuded with the Capulets in *Romeo and Juliet?*

    A The Corleones
    B The Montagues
    C The Borgias

7 In Rhythmic Gymnastics, competitors have four pieces of apparatus: rope, hoop, ball … and what?

    A Baton
    B Ribbon
    C Flower

8 What were the first names of 1950s singing duo the Everly Brothers?

    A Bill and Ben
    B Don and Phil
    C Mike and Ron

9 Who are the children in *The Royle Family*?

    A Denise and Dave
    B Barbara and Anthony
    C Denise and Anthony

10 Where did the Boxer Rising take place?

    A India
    B China
    C The Sudan

11 What did David Prowse and James Earl Jones have in common?

    A Both played the same character in one film
    B Both appeared on Green Cross Code ads
    C Both sang the American anthem at baseball games

12 If an American were wearing a vest, what name would it be given by a British person?

    A Vest
    B Waistcoat
    C Tanktop

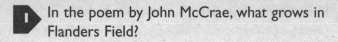

1 In the poem by John McCrae, what grows in Flanders Field?

    A The wheat
    B The grass
    C The poppies

2 What is a trug?

    A An enclosure for pigs
    B A shallow basket
    C A lightweight net

3 What is the most populous city in the world?

    A Beijing
    B Mexico City
    C Cairo

4 David Bowie had a chart success in 1982 with which old crooner?

    A Andy Williams
    B Bing Crosby
    C Dean Martin

5 Which tower in the Tower of London is the original Norman one?

    A Bloody Tower
    B White Tower
    C Bell Tower

6 What English football club plays at The Hawthorns?

    A Wolverhampton Wanderers
    B Birmingham City
    C West Bromwich Albion

7 What is the fraction given to represent pi?

A $^{22}/_7$
B $^{21}/_8$
C $^{27}/_9$

8 What *Are You Being Served?* regular later went on to greater success in *EastEnders*?

A Wendy Richards
B John Inman
C Mollie Sugden

9 What did Yankee Doodle put in his cap?

A A flag
B A feather
C A ticket

10 What movie ends with the line, 'Good, for a minute I thought we were in trouble'?

A *One Flew Over the Cuckoo's Nest*
B *Butch Cassidy and the Sundance Kid*
C *Dr Strangelove*

11 Who composed *The Carnival of the Animals*, the *Organ Symphony* and *Danse Macabre*?

A Ravel
B Debussy
C Saint-Saens

12 Frank Bruno had a top 30 hit at Christmas 1995; what was it?

A *The Greatest Love Of All*
B *Eye Of The Tiger*
C *Punch and Judy*

1 B
2 B
3 A
4 C
5 A
6 B
7 B
8 B
9 C
10 B
11 A
12 B

1 How many Arabian Nights were there?

   A 21
   B 101
   C 1001

2 How many Earth years does it take for Uranus to orbit the sun?

   A 84
   B 25
   C 69

3 What religious cult did American Mary Baker Eddy found?

   A Scientology
   B Christian Science
   C Christian Science Fiction

4 Who won the Champions League in 2003?

   A AC Milan
   B Valencia
   C Barcelona

5 Who was Winnie the Pooh's donkey friend?

   A Hee-haw
   B Eyore
   C Neddy

6 What actor played multiple parts in the classic British film *Kind Hearts And Coronets*?

   A Michael Redgrave
   B Alec Guinness
   C Ralph Richardson

7 What happened to the Asian island of Krakatoa in 1883?

    A It was invaded by Britain
    B Part of it sank after an earthquake
    C Half of it was blown away in a volcanic eruption

8 In Formula One racing, what does a plain black flag mean?

    A The race is being stopped
    B A driver has been injured or killed
    C Michael Schumacher has just won

9 By the end of the millennium, how many times had the UK won the Eurovision Song Contest?

    A 3
    B 5
    C 8

10 What was the name of Edmund Blackadder's sidekick through the ages?

    A Percy
    B Baldrick
    C Darling

11 What is an alloy?

    A A base metal
    B A veneered metal
    C A mixture of metals

12 Who performed the first heart transplant?

    A Christiaan Barnard
    B Patrick Steptoe
    C Alain Carpentier

A
48

1	C
2	B
3	B
4	B
5	B
6	C
7	A
8	A
9	B
10	B
11	C
12	B

1 What is the name given to someone who studies prehistoric life through fossils?

A Archaeologist
B Palaeontologist
C Lepidopterist

2 What dog has pride of place in the Mystery Machine?

A Scooby-Doo
B Muttley
C Droopy

3 What is a billabong?

A A tin can
B A creek
C A hat with corks hanging from the brim

4 What killed 20 million people in Europe in 1918–19?

A Ethnic struggles
B War injuries
C Flu

5 'Don't Give Away The Ending… It's The Only One We Have'. What film was this advertising?

A *The Sixth Sense*
B *Psycho*
C *Carrie*

6 What British fashion designer took over as director of Christian Dior in 1990?

A Stella McCartney
B Alexander McQueen
C John Galliano

7 What club won the FA Premiership and Cup double in 1998?

   A Manchester Utd
   B Arsenal
   C Leeds Utd

8 Where did singer Natalie Imbruglia get her big break?

   A On *Neighbours*
   B In the Australian charts
   C On ads for Vegemite

9 Who was the first woman to be elected MP in Britain?

   A Constance Markiewicz
   B Nancy Astor
   C Margaret Bondfield

10 What was Bangladesh before it got its present name in 1971?

   A East Pakistan
   B West Pakistan
   C A part of India

11 Who wrote *The Pilgrim's Progress*?

   A John Milton
   B John Donne
   C John Bunyan

12 Which of these colours does not appear on the flag of the Czech Republic?

   A Red
   B Yellow
   C Blue

A 49

1	C
2	A
3	B
4	A
5	B
6	B
7	C
8	A
9	B
10	B
11	C
12	A

1 In what city did Anne Frank and her family hide out from the Nazis?

   A Rotterdam
   B Amsterdam
   C Potsdam

2 What is the Mercalli Scale used to measure?

   A Barometric pressure
   B Density of elements
   C Earthquake intensity

3 Apart from Marc Bolan, who was the other half of 70s pop duo T Rex?

   A Mickey Took
   B Mickey Finn
   C Mickey Feld

4 What creature does the Anglo-Saxon warrior Beowulf slay?

   A The Green Knight
   B The Green Dragon
   C Grendel

5 On the map of the London Underground, what line is coloured yellow?

   A Central
   B District
   C Circle

6 How much of the ball has to cross the goal-line for a goal to be awarded in football?

   A Any part of the ball
   B Most of the ball
   C The entire ball

7 What was American gangster Al Capone eventually jailed for?

    A Bootlegging
    B Ordering the St Valentine's Day Massacre
    C Tax evasion

8 Where would you be most likely to see the letters http?

    A On your medical records
    B On your computer
    C On your tax coding

9 How did Samantha, the central character in the 1960s sitcom *Bewitched*, work her magic?

    A Waved her wand
    B Pointed her finger
    C Wiggled her nose

10 When is Passiontide?

    A The last week of Lent
    B The last week of Lent and week after Easter
    C The last two weeks of Lent

11 As well as in the film *White Christmas*, Bing Crosby sang this title song in what other film?

    A *Going My Way*
    B *Holiday Inn*
    C *The Road To Alaska*

12 What scientist wrote the bestselling *A Brief History of Time*?

    A Carl Sagan
    B Jacob Bronowski
    C Stephen Hawking

A 50

1	B
2	A
3	B
4	C
5	B
6	C
7	B
8	A
9	A
10	A
11	C
12	B

1 What political party introduced the Old Age Pension?

    A Labour
    B Conservatives
    C Liberals

2 Tammy Wynette had a hit with *Justified And Ancient* in 1991. Who was she singing with?

    A KLF
    B REM
    C XTC

3 What is the name of a golf stroke that is two under par for the hole?

    A Birdie
    B Bogey
    C Eagle

4 What would you do with winkle-pickers?

    A Wear them
    B Extract crustaceans with them
    C Arrange flowers with them

5 What Hollywood director and writer directed an episode of ER?

    A Martin Scorsese
    B Ron Howard
    C Quentin Tarantino

6 What day marked the end of the Celtic year?

    A Halloween
    B Midwinter's Eve
    C The eve of the Spring Equinox

7 Who, apart from Italy and France, has hosted the World Cup twice?

    A Brazil
    B Mexico
    C Chile

8 Who was the last tsar of Russia?

    A Alexander II
    B Nicholas II
    C Grigori II

9 What witch was killed when Dorothy's house fell on her in *The Wizard of Oz*?

    A West
    B North
    C East

10 Who wrote *The Wind In The Willows*?

    A A.A. Milne
    B Kenneth Grahame
    C C.S. Lewis

11 What country is the world's most sparsely populated?

    A Micronesia
    B Greenland
    C Iceland

12 At 2% of the body's weight, how much of the body's energy does the brain use up?

    A 5%
    B 12%
    C 20%

A

51

1 B
2 C
3 B
4 C
5 C
6 C
7 C
8 B
9 C
10 C
11 B
12 C

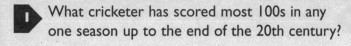

Q U E S T I O N S

53

1 What cricketer has scored most 100s in any one season up to the end of the 20th century?

    A W.G. Grace
    B Denis Compton
    C Gary Sobers

2 How many cents are there in a US nickel?

    A 5
    B 10
    C 25

3 What is an astrolabe?

    A An Earth-orbiting space station
    B An instrument used in astronomy
    C A communication device used on spacewalks

4 Who were *Young, Gifted and Black* in 1970?

    A Bob & Earl
    B Bob & Donna
    C Bob & Marcia

5 In the Army, what is a WO?

    A Woman Officer
    B Warrant Officer
    C Washroom Orderly

6 What date is St George's Day?

    A February 23
    B April 23
    C June 23

7 What was the second-greatest computer ever in *The Hitch-Hiker's Guide To The Galaxy*?

  A Deep Thought
  B Big Brain
  C Baby

8 Who played the school head in *The Belles Of St Trinian's*?

  A Margaret Rutherford
  B Alastair Sim
  C Joyce Grenfell

9 How much silver must an item be made of to gain a hallmark?

  A 78%
  B 92.5%
  C 100%

10 What New England town was the scene of infamous witch-hunts in the 17th century?

  A Boston
  B Plymouth
  C Salem

11 How many marriages featured in the final wedding scene in *Seven Brides For Seven Brothers*?

  A 6
  B 7
  C 8

12 How many men did the *Grand Old Duke Of York* have?

  A One Thousand
  B Five Thousand
  C Ten Thousand

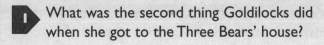
1 What was the second thing Goldilocks did when she got to the Three Bears' house?

A Lay on the beds
B Sat on the chairs
C Ate the porridge

2 What is Hansen's disease more commonly known as?

A Infantilism
B Piles
C Leprosy

3 Who was the Franciscan monk with the inquiring mind in *The Name Of The Rose*?

A Brother Sherlock
B Brother Mycroft
C Brother William of Baskerville

4 What country has won more gold medals than any other in the modern Olympic Games?

A Soviet Union
B USA
C Germany (East & West)

5 What Tears For Fears single was a US number 1 and won a Brit Award for Best Single?

A *Change*
B *Shout*
C *Everybody Wants To Rule The World*

6 Which of the following was not a Roman emperor?

A Probus
B Pertinax
C Epheseus

7 Where was the American naval base Pearl Harbor?

    A Washington State
    B Hawaii
    C San Diego

8 Whose forecast in 1984 was *It's Raining Men*?

    A Weather Men
    B Weather Girls
    C Weather Prophets

9 What name is given to a car built between 1919 and 1930?

    A Vintage
    B Veteran
    C Banger

10 What was Inspector Morse's first name?

    A Endeavour
    B Pagan
    C Honest

11 To the nearest mile, how long is Hadrian's Wall?

    A 54 miles
    B 66 miles
    C 73 miles

12 The Marcus-Nelson Murders movie introduced what popular 70s detective for the first time?

    A *Shaft*
    B *Colombo*
    C *Kojak*

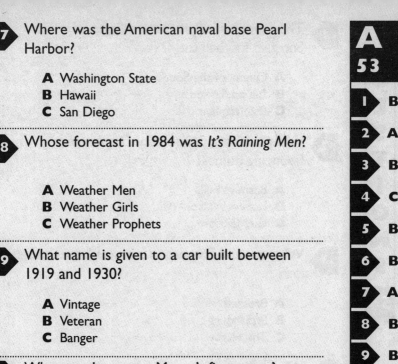

A
53

1	B
2	A
3	B
4	C
5	B
6	B
7	A
8	B
9	B
10	C
11	A
12	C

1 The Doonhamers is the nickname of what Scottish football team?

A Queen of the South
B Albion Rovers
C Dunfermline

2 What inventor devised the Dambusters' bouncing bombs?

A Barnes Wallis
B Robert Watson-Watt
C Guy Gibson

3 Where is the European Court of Justice based?

A Brussels
B Strasbourg
C The Hague

4 What was the first-ever wholly computer-generated film?

A *Star Wars*
B *Toy Story*
C *Snow White And The Seven Dwarfs*

5 What year did daily rum rations stop in the Royal Navy?

A 1740
B 1890
C 1970

6 What country had the first woman prime minister?

A Sri Lanka
B Israel
C UK

7 What monkey is the only one with a blood factor also found in human blood?

   A Chimpanzee
   B Rhesus
   C Gorilla

8 In the language of flowers, what plant represents egotism?

   A Fern
   B Mistletoe
   C Narcissus

9 Who was the third son of Adam and Eve?

   A Abel
   B Seth
   C Cain

10 What children's story features a giant who smells the blood of an Englishman?

   A *The Selfish Giant*
   B *Jack And The Beanstalk*
   C *The BFG*

11 What relation were Richard and Karen Carpenter?

   A Husband and wife
   B They weren't related
   C Brother and sister

12 What was the name of the story and film that featured the Mobile Army Surgical Hospital?

   A *Good Morning, Vietnam*
   B *Catch 22*
   C *M*A*S*H*

A
54

1	B
2	C
3	C
4	B
5	C
6	C
7	B
8	B
9	A
10	A
11	C
12	C

1 What national side does footballer Rivaldo play for?

A Italy
B Brazil
C Spain

2 How many pennies were there in a pre-decimal pound?

A 240
B 120
C 160

3 What position did Alfred Lord Tennyson hold from 1850 to 1896?

A Foreign Secretary
B Poet Laureate
C First president of the RSPCA

4 Where are the Aran Islands?

A Off the west coast of Ireland
B Off the west coast of Scotland
C Off the coast of Northumbria

5 What famous fictional detective first appeared in *The Mysterious Affair At Styles*?

A Hercule Poirot
B Miss Marple
C Lord Peter Wimsey

6 What do Americans call Old Glory?

A A geyser in Yellowstone Park
B The American Flag
C The Statue of Liberty

7 What nationality is country singer Shania Twain?

  A Canadian
  B American
  C Swiss

8 If someone was panhandling in North America, what would they be doing?

  A Cooking
  B Prospecting
  C Begging

9 Who actually said, 'A man's gotta do what a man's gotta do'?

  A James Cagney
  B Alan Ladd
  C John Wayne

10 Who was the only horse to win the Grand National three times?

  A Golden Miller
  B Desert Orchid
  C Red Rum

11 What did Paul Scott's series of novels, *The Raj Quartet*, make it to TV as?

  A *Heat and Dust*
  B *A Passage to India*
  C *The Jewel in the Crown*

12 What is Madonna's surname?

  A Riggione
  B Antoni
  C Ciccone

1 What was the actress Diana Fluck better known as?

    A Diana Dors
    B Diana Rigg
    C Diana Quick

2 How many bytes are in a kilobyte?

    A 1000
    B 1024
    C 1048

3 One-hit wonders Fiddlers Dram had a UK Christmas hit in 1979 with what song?

    A *I Am A Cider Drinker*
    B *Mouldy Old Dough*
    C *Day Trip To Bangor*

4 What Shakespearean play do actors think it bad luck to name?

    A Macbeth
    B King Lear
    C Richard III

5 What took place on 4 July 1776?

    A The Bastille was stormed in Paris
    B The United Irishmen revolt began
    C America signed the Declaration of Independence

6 What year would an American sophomore student be in?

    A First
    B Second
    C Third

7 Who won consecutive baseball gold medals in the first two Olympic Games to feature the sport?

    A USA
    B Cuba
    C Japan

8 What country is the Canadian River in?

    A USA
    B Australia
    C Canada

9 What Bond film did the Bondgirl Mary Goodnight appear in?

    A *The Man With The Golden Gun*
    B *Diamonds Are Forever*
    C *Moonraker*

10 What ship carried Francis Drake on his round-the-world voyage of 1577-80?

    A The Cutty Sark
    B The Marie Rose
    C The Golden Hind

11 What is the fifth book of the New Testament?

    A Romans
    B Revelation
    C The Acts of the Apostles

12 Whose horse was called Hercules?

    A Roy Rogers
    B Steptoe and Son's
    C Zorro's

A
56

1	B
2	A
3	B
4	A
5	A
6	B
7	A
8	C
9	B
10	C
11	C
12	C

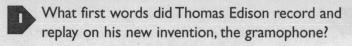

1 What first words did Thomas Edison record and replay on his new invention, the gramophone?

    A God bless the United States of America
    B Mary had a little lamb
    C Get me to the patent office

2 What colour is puce?

    A Sickly green
    B Dark red
    C Chocolate brown

3 What cricketer scored most runs in any one day, up to the end of the 20th century?

    A Gary Sobers
    B Ian Botham
    C Brian Lara

4 What unusual physical marking does Harry Potter have?

    A A broomstick-shaped birthmark on his shoulder
    B A lightning-bolt shaped scar on his forehead
    C An extra little finger on his left hand

5 Two countries share the island of Hispaniola. One is Haiti; what is the other?

    A Dominican Republic
    B Puerto Rico
    C Grenada

6 What do k.d. lang's initials stand for?

    A Karen Drusilla
    B Kathy Dawn
    C Katrina Donna

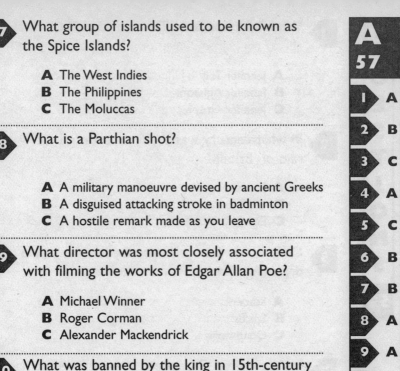

7 What group of islands used to be known as the Spice Islands?

    A The West Indies
    B The Philippines
    C The Moluccas

8 What is a Parthian shot?

    A A military manoeuvre devised by ancient Greeks
    B A disguised attacking stroke in badminton
    C A hostile remark made as you leave

9 What director was most closely associated with filming the works of Edgar Allan Poe?

    A Michael Winner
    B Roger Corman
    C Alexander Mackendrick

10 What was banned by the king in 15th-century Scotland for interfering with archery practice?

    A Golf
    B Football
    C Whisky drinking

11 What sitcom pairing shared a flat in Nelson Mandela House?

    A Del Boy and Rodney Trotter
    B Gary and Tony
    C Victor and Margaret Meldrew

12 What musical was based on the Federico Fellini movie 8½?

    A Nine
    B I Love My Wife
    C House Of Flowers

A
57

1 A
2 B
3 C
4 A
5 C
6 B
7 B
8 A
9 A
10 C
11 C
12 B

1 Who did actor Brad Pitt marry in 2000?

A Jennifer Tilly
B Jennifer Aniston
C Jennifer Grey

2 In what century was the first recorded Viking raid on Britain?

A Fourth
B Sixth
C Eighth

3 Oxford was famously described as the 'city of dreaming...' what?

A Students
B Spires
C Quadrangles

4 In Washington, DC, one in every 25 people has the same profession. What is it?

A Politician
B Civil servant
C Lawyer

5 On what island is John F. Kennedy International Airport?

A Manhattan
B Staten Island
C Long Island

6 What 1946 film featured heavenly scenes in monochrome and scenes on earth in colour?

A *It's A Wonderful Life*
B *A Matter Of Life And Death*
C *The Seventh Veil*

7 What name is given to a type of toxin produced by a plant?

   A Zootoxin
   B Ecotoxin
   C Phytotoxin

8 Thor, the Norse god of thunder, carried a magical article in his hand. What was it?

   A A wand
   B A thunderbolt
   C A hammer

9 How many hands has Big Ben?

   A 8
   B 2
   C 0

10 Who scored a memorable hit in 1984 with *Agadoo*?

   A Black Lace
   B Bucks Fizz
   C Brotherhood of Man

11 What family's cartoon show do Itchy and Scratchy regularly appear on?

   A *The Addams*
   B *The Flintstones*
   C *The Simpsons*

12 In Scrabble, which two letters are worth 10 points?

   A Q and Z
   B J and X
   C V and Y

1 What was the last year when a British player won a singles title at Wimbledon?

    A 1977
    B 1936
    C 1952

2 What is Schadenfreude?

    A German fairytale character with pointed fingers
    B Pleasure in someone else's bad luck
    C The ability to move objects by willpower

3 What was Abba's last UK number 1?

    A *Thank You For The Music*
    B *Super Trouper*
    C *The Day Before You Came*

4 When was the first nonstop transatlantic flight?

    A 1935
    B 1931
    C 1927

5 What is the world's longest river?

    A The Nile
    B The Yangtze
    C The Amazon

6 In the movie *The Incredible Shrinking Man*, what causes the man to shrink?

    A An experimental potion he swallowed
    B A ray gun he stood in front of
    C A radioactive fog he passed through

7 Who first described his achievements with the words 'Standing on the shoulders of giants'?

  A Isaac Newton
  B Bernard of Chartres
  C Noel Gallagher

8 How many inches are in a square foot?

  A 12
  B 48
  C 144

9 Who or what were Gog and Magog?

  A Two Biblical cities destroyed by God's wrath
  B Two Ancient Egyptian gods
  C The last two survivors of a race of British giants

10 What metal is combined with tin to create bronze?

  A Copper
  B Iron
  C Gold

11 What cult TV show features a nightclub called the Bronze?

  A *Buffy the Vampire Slayer*
  B *Roswell High*
  C *Dawson's Creek*

12 What happens on the 'Glorious Twelfth'?

  A Orangemen march through Belfast
  B The grouse-shooting season begins
  C The 12 days of Christmas end

1	**B**
2	**C**
3	**B**
4	**C**
5	**C**
6	**B**
7	**C**
8	**C**
9	**C**
10	**A**
11	**C**
12	**A**

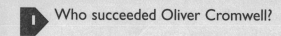

Q U E S T I O N S 61

1 Who succeeded Oliver Cromwell?

  A Charles II
  B Cromwell's son, Richard
  C Parliament took power

2 What type of rock is coal found in?

  A Cretaceous
  B Cambrian
  C Carboniferous

3 What Brit made his directorial debut on *Oh What A Lovely War!?*

  A Michael Winner
  B Lindsay Anderson
  C Richard Attenborough

4 What creature is always chased by Wyle E. Coyote?

  A The Roadrunner
  B Tweety Pie
  C Bugs Bunny

5 What is the highest civilian merit award in the UK?

  A The George Cross
  B The Victoria Cross
  C The Order of Merit

6 What was the D'Oyly Carte Opera Company founded to stage?

  A The works of Verdi
  B The works of Gilbert and Sullivan
  C The works of Mozart

7 What was the first university in Britain?

    A Oxford
    B Cambridge
    C St Andrews

8 Jesus's Apostles each have a pictorial representation. What is used to represent Peter?

    A A fish
    B A cockerel
    C Crossed keys

9 In Scotland, what is a broch?

    A A fortified tower
    B A thick and creamy soup
    C A lament played on the bagpipes

10 When were Manchester United last relegated?

    A 1972
    B 1973
    C 1974

11 What monster made his film debut in 1955 and has appeared often since?

    A Godzilla
    B Taz the Tasmanian Devil
    C King Kong

12 *Maggie May*, Rod Stewart's first number 1, was a double A-side. What was on the other side?

    A *What Made Milwaukee Famous*
    B *You Wear It Well*
    C *Reason to Believe*

A
60

1 ▸ A
2 ▸ B
3 ▸ B
4 ▸ C
5 ▸ A
6 ▸ C
7 ▸ B
8 ▸ C
9 ▸ C
10 ▸ A
11 ▸ A
12 ▸ B

1 What city was the birthplace of Wolfgang Amadeus Mozart?

   A Vienna
   B Salzburg
   C Prague

2 What 1890 innovation made football easier to play?

   A Goal nets
   B Shinguards
   C Floodlights

3 All the King Jameses in Britain belonged to one royal house; what was it?

   A Bruce
   B Tudor
   C Stewart

4 In musical notes, what relation does a quaver have to a crotchet?

   A It is half as long
   B It is twice as long
   C It is one note up from a crotchet

5 What historical event was portrayed by the movie *They Died With Their Boots On*?

   A The Charge of The Light Brigade
   B The Battle of the Little Big Horn
   C The Battle of Gettysburg

6 Why did the 1926 General Strike take place?

   A So the miners could avoid pay cuts
   B So the miners could force nationalisation
   C So the miners could bring down the government

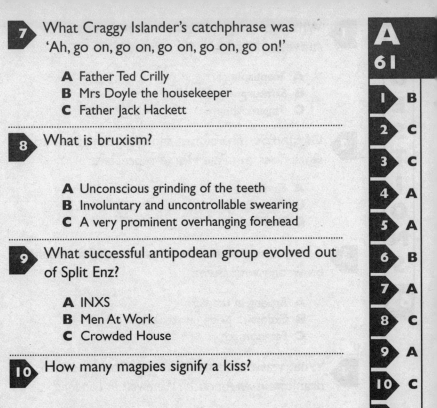

7 What Craggy Islander's catchphrase was 'Ah, go on, go on, go on, go on, go on!'

    A Father Ted Crilly
    B Mrs Doyle the housekeeper
    C Father Jack Hackett

8 What is bruxism?

    A Unconscious grinding of the teeth
    B Involuntary and uncontrollable swearing
    C A very prominent overhanging forehead

9 What successful antipodean group evolved out of Split Enz?

    A INXS
    B Men At Work
    C Crowded House

10 How many magpies signify a kiss?

    A 2
    B 4
    C 9

11 What US state is bordered by the Mississippi on the west and the Missouri on the east?

    A Iowa
    B Missouri
    C Minnesota

12 Which of the following stars was not born in Britain?

    A Bob Hope
    B Grace Kelly
    C Cary Grant

A
61

1 B
2 C
3 C
4 A
5 A
6 B
7 A
8 C
9 A
10 C
11 A
12 C

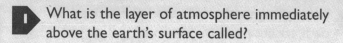

1 What is the layer of atmosphere immediately above the earth's surface called?

   A Troposphere
   B Stratosphere
   C Thermosphere

2 Of the Four Horsemen of the Apocalypse, what does the Pale Horse represent?

   A Famine
   B The triumph of the power of Good over Evil
   C Death

3 If someone suffered from tympany, what would be wrong with them?

   A Ringing in the ears
   B Excessive pride or arrogance
   C Fat stomach

4 What was the name of the pub the Americans drank in in *An American Werewolf In London*?

   A The Slaughtered Lamb
   B The Dead Sheep
   C The Scary Shepherd

5 What 1960s comedy show had a butler called Lurch?

   A *The Addams Family*
   B *The Munsters*
   C *I Dream Of Jeannie*

6 What future king built the Royal Pavilion at Brighton?

   A George III
   B George IV
   C George V

7 How many players does the fielding team have on a cricket pitch?

A 11
B 13
C 15

8 What decade saw the first Labour government voted into office?

A 1910s
B 1920s
C 1930s

9 What charismatic lead singer played Shelley in Corman's 1990 movie *Frankenstein Unbound*?

A Mick Jagger
B Bryan Ferry
C Michael Hutchence

10 When was the Atlantic first crossed by a manned balloon flight?

A 1878
B 1928
C 1978

11 In what trade did Hepplewhite, Chippendale, Kent and Sheraton make their names?

A Painting
B Running top-class London hotels
C Making furniture

12 What is the world's most populous predominantly Muslim country?

A Pakistan
B Indonesia
C Saudi Arabia

131

1 Major Pat Reid's wartime experiences became a book, TV series and film; what were they called?

A *The Colditz Story*
B *U-571*
C *The Dam Busters*

2 In World War II, what manoeuvre was Operation Dynamo better known as?

A The Normandy landings
B The Italian campaign
C The Dunkirk evacuation

3 What planet has a moon called Titan?

A Jupiter
B Saturn
C Neptune

4 At what time do monks attend vespers?

A Before dawn
B Late morning
C Early evening

5 Who took the lead role in the 1962 movie *Bird Man Of Alcatraz*?

A Steve McQueen
B Burt Lancaster
C Clint Eastwood

6 Who was the 20th century's youngest England football player?

A Michael Owen
B Gary Lineker
C Bobby Charlton

7 Not including continents, what is the world's largest island?

    A Greenland
    B Borneo
    C New Guinea

8 What type of dive is allowed only in platform diving?

    A Armstand
    B Reverse
    C Twist

9 What was Bon Jovi's first UK top 20 hit?

    A *Hardest Part Is The Night*
    B *Livin' On A Prayer*
    C *You Give Love A Bad Name*

10 The English town of Boston is in what county?

    A Leicestershire
    B Lincolnshire
    C Northamptonshire

11 The American city of Boston is in what state?

    A New Hampshire
    B Massachusetts
    C Maine

12 Who was the first American to orbit the Earth?

    A Neil Armstrong
    B Buzz Aldrin
    C John Glenn

A
63

1	A
2	C
3	B
4	A
5	A
6	B
7	A
8	B
9	C
10	C
11	C
12	B

1 Which of the following is not a shipping area around Britain's coast?

    A Norway
    B Sole
    C Bailey

2 What is the basic ingredient in hummus?

    A Anchovies
    B Chickpeas
    C Aubergine

3 What town would you visit to see the Bayeux Tapestry?

    A Bayeux
    B London
    C Paris

4 Which of the following footballing bodies was founded first?

    A Football League
    B Football Association
    C Irish League

5 What single engagement cost the British Army over 400,000 casualties?

    A The Battle of Waterloo, 1815
    B The Battle of the Somme, 1916
    C The Battle of Britain, 1940

6 How many times did Christopher Columbus sail to the New World?

    A Two
    B Three
    C Four

7 Who were the first English County cricket champions, in 1890?

   A Middlesex
   B Surrey
   C Sussex

8 What would you normally find in a bandbox?

   A Musical instruments
   B Hats
   C Men's neckties

9 Shakin' Stevens had a 1981 hit with *This Old House*. Who had a hit with it in the 50s?

   A Bing Crosby
   B Doris Day
   C Rosemary Clooney

10 What planet does *Dr Who* come from?

   A Earth
   B Gallifrey
   C Mars

11 In the movie *Time After Time*, Jack The Ripper is chased through time – by what character?

   A Sherlock Holmes
   B Edward, Prince of Wales
   C H.G. Wells

12 Snakes are the symbol of what saint?

   A St Patrick
   B St Francis of Assisi
   C St George

1 What French singer's surname translates as 'little sparrow'?

A Charles Aznavour
B Sacha Distel
C Edith Piaf

2 What city is ER's Cook County General Memorial Hospital set in?

A Chicago
B Boston
C New York

3 The Douglas Coupland book *Girlfriend In A Coma* takes its name from a song by what band?

A New Order
B Pulp
C The Smiths

4 What feat was Francis Drake the first Englishman to achieve?

A Winning a bowling match against the Spanish
B Sailing around the world
C Becoming the lover of Queen Elizabeth

5 What is the biggest of the 10 National Parks in England and Wales?

A Lake District
B Snowdonia
C Yorkshire Dales

6 Who is included in the FT Ordinary Share Index?

A The top 30 UK companies
B The next 30 UK companies outside the FT-SE 100
C 30 companies representative of UK industry

7 What are the brightest stars of the constellation Ursa Major better known as?

   A The Great Bear
   B The Plough
   C The Southern Cross

8 What are Codling, Blenheim and Laxton?

   A University colleges
   B Types of apple
   C Types of fish

9 What is the world's longest bridge?

   A Akashi-Kaikyo in Japan
   B Bosporus in Turkey
   C Humber in England

10 What was Princess Leia's home planet, destroyed by the Death Star in *Star Wars*?

   A Hoth
   B Tatooine
   C Alderaan

11 What part of a river is the delta?

   A A river mouth with many streams
   B A river's flood plain
   C A stranded lake, not part of the river any more

12 Which American sport do the Green Bay Packers, San Francisco 49ers and Chicago Bears play?

   A American football
   B Basketball
   C Baseball

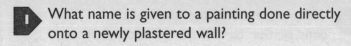

1 What name is given to a painting done directly onto a newly plastered wall?

- **A** Fresco
- **B** Tondo
- **C** Frieze

2 What Irish port was formerly named Queenstown?

- **A** Dun Laoghaire
- **B** Cobh
- **C** Rosslare

3 What was the nickname of Marillion's lead singer?

- **A** Pork
- **B** Chicken
- **C** Fish

4 What is the only animated feature film ever to be nominated for a Best Picture Oscar?

- **A** *Snow White and the Seven Dwarfs*
- **B** *Beauty and the Beast*
- **C** *Toy Story*

5 Who played Quentin Crisp in the TV production of *The Naked Civil Servant*?

- **A** John Inman
- **B** John Hurt
- **C** John Malkovich

6 Why did Manchester United pull out of the FA Cup in the season 1999–2000?

- **A** They were too tired
- **B** To play in the World Club Championship
- **C** To give someone else a chance

7 What member of the Apollo 11 team did not land on the moon?

    A John Glenn
    B Buzz Aldrin
    C Michael Collins

8 If you were 10 fathoms under the sea, how deep would you be?

    A 60 feet
    B 60 yards
    C 600 yards

9 What is Ash Wednesday the start of?

    A Spring
    B The Easter Season
    C Lent

10 What design classic was created by Harry Beck?

    A The London Underground map
    B The Gill Sans typeface
    C The Coca-Cola bottle

11 Who was the 'turbulent priest', later to be martyred, that Henry II demanded to be rid of?

    A Thomas à Becket
    B Thomas More
    C Thomas Aquinas

12 Who invented the mini-skirt?

    A Zandra Rhodes
    B Vivienne Westwood
    C Mary Quant

A
66

1   C
2   A
3   C
4   B
5   A
6   C
7   B
8   B
9   A
10   C
11   A
12   A

1 Who invented the first flush lavatory?

  A William Shanks
  B Thomas Crapper
  C Sir John Harrington

2 Who had a hit with their *Instant Karma* in 1970?

  A Lennon, Ono and the Plastic Ono Band
  B John Lennon and Yoko Ono
  C John Lennon with the Plastic Ono Band

3 What is a five-faced bishop?

  A A particularly duplicitous clergyman
  B A plant
  C A town clock

4 Where would you expect to find a piscina?

  A In a lavatory
  B At the harbourside
  C Near a church altar

5 Who was the leader of the 1605 Gunpowder Plot to blow up the Houses of Parliament?

  A Robert Catesby
  B Guy Fawkes
  C Thomas Winter

6 How long is a goalkeeper allowed to hold the ball?

  A 4 seconds
  B 5 seconds
  C 6 seconds

7 What chemical element is represented by the symbol Au?

   A Aluminium
   B Gold
   C Scandium

8 The River Rhine flows through three countries: Germany, Switzerland … and what?

   A France
   B Netherlands
   C Belgium

9 What musical had the line, 'Blossom of snow, may you bloom and grow, Bloom and grow for ever'?

   A *Song of Norway*
   B *The Sound of Music*
   C *The Maid of the Mountains*

10 In the *Watch With Mother* puppet show, what was the name of the Woodentops' dog?

   A Floppy Dog
   B Spotty Dog
   C Woody Dog

11 In medieval times, what was a man's destrier and a woman's palfrey?

   A Servant
   B Coat of arms
   C Horse

12 Who provocatively told the Americans after winning his 1982 Oscar, 'The British are coming!'?

   A David Puttnam
   B Colin Welland
   C Hugh Hudson

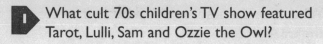

1 What cult 70s children's TV show featured Tarot, Lulli, Sam and Ozzie the Owl?

A Ace of Wands
B The Tomorrow People
C Timeslip

2 Who is Eric Arthur Blair better known as?

A Tony Blair
B George Orwell
C Jarvis Cocker

3 In the birthday rhyme that begins, Monday's child is fair of face; what is said of Thursday's child?

A Has far to go
B Is bonny and blithe, good and gay
C Is loving and giving

4 If someone's interest is errinophily, what would they be interested in?

A All kinds of stamps except postage stamps
B Blunders, especially made by the civil service
C Anything related to Ireland

5 Why is the Mediterranean island of Stromboli famous?

A For its active volcano
B Because Roman emperors used to holiday there
C For its intact Roman remains

6 Whose baby is baptised at the end of *The Godfather*?

A Michael and Kay's
B Connie and Carlo's
C Sonny and Deanna's

7 Who were the first Scottish band ever to top the UK charts?

    A Middle of the Road
    B Marmalade
    C Bay City Rollers

8 In a lunar month, how many phases does the moon have?

    A 1
    B 2
    C 4

9 In canoeing and kayaking, what is meant by the jargon term 'Eskimo roll'?

    A Whale-blubber sandwich
    B Circular lifebelt
    C Self-righting technique in an overturned boat

10 What document was drawn up by the nobility to outline their grievances against King John?

    A Domesday Book
    B Magna Carta
    C Bayeux Tapestry

11 What was the name of Vivienne Westwood and Malcolm McLaren's 1970s King's Road shop?

    A Sex
    B Bondage
    C Pistols

12 What was the only building from the 1951 Festival of Britain designed to last?

    A The Dome of Discovery
    B The Royal Festival Hall
    C The Skylon Obelisk

A
68

1	C
2	A
3	B
4	C
5	A
6	C
7	B
8	B
9	B
10	B
11	C
12	B

1 On the Beaufort scale of wind speeds, what wind speed has a force 9 strong gale?

   A 47–54 mph
   B 55–63 mph
   C 64–75 mph

2 What film was made from the book *Do Androids Dream Of Electric Sheep?*

   A *Electric Dreams*
   B *Blade Runner*
   C *Fahrenheit 451*

3 What US band had a hit single on both sides of the Atlantic with *American Girl*?

   A Survivor
   B REO Speedwagon
   C Tom Petty and the Heartbreakers

4 Whose motto is Honi Soit Qui Mal Y Pense (Evil To Him Who Evil Thinks)?

   A The Lifeguards
   B The Knights of the Round Table
   C The Order of the Garter

5 What are Great Helm, Basinet and Lobster Tail all types of?

   A Armoured helmet
   B Seagull
   C Fishing boat

6 How many plagues were sent to punish the ancient Egyptians?

   A 4
   B 10
   C 12

7 In athletics track events, what is the longest sprint race?

    A 200m
    B 400m
    C 800m

8 Whose catchphrase was 'I have a cunning plan'?

    A René in *Allo, Allo*
    B Private Pike in *Dad's Army*
    C Baldrick in *Blackadder*

9 What name is given to plants that flower year after year?

    A Perennials
    B Annuals
    C Hardy annuals

10 How was Edward IV's rebel brother George, Duke of Clarence, said to have been murdered?

    A Drowned in a butt of wine
    B Skewered with a poker
    C Left to rot in a dungeon in the Tower of London

11 What is the longest river in the British Isles?

    A Thames
    B Shannon
    C Clyde

12 The daughter of singing star Don Everly married another singer in 1990; who was he?

    A Michael Stipe
    B Jon Bon Jovi
    C Axl Rose

1 What chameleon-like star was known as the Thin White Duke?

    A Johnny Rotten
    B David Bowie
    C Marc Bolan

2 What symbol of the Zodiac is represented by an archer?

    A Libra
    B Sagittarius
    C Gemini

3 What book of the Bible comes after Genesis?

    A Deuteronomy
    B Numbers
    C Exodus

4 Who had a top 20 hit with *He Was Beautiful*, theme from the movie *The Deer Hunter*?

    A Iris Williams
    B John Williams
    C Andy Williams

5 What was the first North European football team to win the European Cup?

    A PSV Eindhoven
    B Bayern Munich
    C Celtic

6 What would a fletcher's profession have been?

    A Making barrels
    B Butchery
    C Making arrows

7 What London pub is mentioned in *Pop Goes The Weasel?*

    A The Monkey
    B The Eagle
    C The Rose and Crown

8 Who wrote the opera *La Traviata?*

    A Verdi
    B Puccini
    C Rossini

9 What king led the English army to a stunning victory against the French at Agincourt in 1415?

    A Henry VI
    B Henry V
    C Henry IV

10 In the famous equation $E = mc^2$, what is c?

    A Carbon
    B The speed of light
    C An atom

11 In the movie *Invasion Of The Body Snatchers*, how do the aliens plan to take over the earth?

    A By replacing people with replicants
    B By controlling people's minds
    C By wiping people out with a lethal organism

12 What group of people did Edward I expel from England in 1290?

    A The Jews
    B The French
    C The Scots

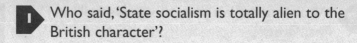

1 Who said, 'State socialism is totally alien to the British character'?

    A Tony Blair
    B Margaret Thatcher
    C Mikhail Gorbachev

2 What is the American name for the constellation The Plough?

    A The Bat
    B The Big Dipper
    C The Kite

3 Who was the first white UK act to be signed by the Tamla Motown label?

    A Lisa Stansfield
    B Bonnie Tyler
    C Kiki Dee

4 What airport is the world's busiest?

    A New York JFK
    B London Heathrow
    C Amsterdam Schiphol

5 Who are known as oppidans?

    A Eton pupils
    B First-time MPs
    C Candidates for the priesthood

6 What would a New Zealander call a Wild Irishman?

    A A whiskey and stout cocktail
    B A thorny native bush
    C A southerly force 9 gale

7 Who were the last team to win football's old First Division championship in 1992?

   A Arsenal
   B Manchester Utd
   C Leeds Utd

8 In what islands are Scapa Flow and the Old Man of Hoy?

   A Shetland
   B Orkney
   C The Hebrides

9 Who played Henry VIII in the movie *A Man For All Seasons*?

   A Paul Scofield
   B Robert Shaw
   C Orson Welles

10 Which of the following has never been a king in Britain?

   A David
   B Edmund
   C Herbert

11 What Danish expression is the word Lego a contraction of?

   A I Play
   B Play Well
   C Build & Play

12 Who was the second president of the United States?

   A George Washington
   B Thomas Jefferson
   C John Adams

1	B
2	B
3	C
4	A
5	C
6	C
7	B
8	A
9	B
10	B
11	A
12	A

149

1 What activity do Horizontal Slow Rolls, Stall Turns and Tail Slides all feature in?

    A Synchronised Swimming
    B Aerobatics
    C Three-day Eventing

2 Actor Brinsley Forde from TV's *The Double Deckers* went on to form what number 1 band?

    A Aswad
    B The Specials
    C The Real Thing

3 What is freezing point in Fahrenheit?

    A 0°
    B 24°
    C 32°

4 What monarch did the Pope reward for loyalty with the title Defender of the Faith in 1521?

    A Mary, Queen of Scots
    B Henry VIII
    C Mary I of England

5 What would you keep locked in a tantalus?

    A Alcohol or wine bottles
    B Medicines
    C Jewellery

6 What country is the district of Picardy in?

    A Belgium
    B France
    C Netherlands

7 Who first introduced tobacco into Europe?

    A Walter Raleigh
    B Francis Drake
    C Christopher Columbus

8 What is a Capuchin?

    A A large coffee
    B A monk
    C A bell-tower

9 What cause did Emily Davison die for as she grabbed the king's horse at the 1913 Derby?

    A Animal rights
    B Anti-monarchy
    C Votes for women

10 What musical did the song *Secret Love* come from?

    A *Calamity Jane*
    B *Oklahoma!*
    C *South Pacific*

11 In what German city is the Brandenburg Gate?

    A Berlin
    B Bonn
    C Brandenburg

12 If an American was described as having bangs, what might you expect to see on their head?

    A Bruises
    B A fringe
    C Big ears

1 Who in the 1980s had a minor UK hit and a huge US one with the song Jesse's Girl?

   A Rick Springfield
   B John Cougar Mellencamp
   C Steve Winwood

2 Which of the three Canadian prairie provinces is furthest west?

   A Alberta
   B Manitoba
   C Saskatchewan

3 When does a ship fly the blue peter signal flag?

   A When it's about to leave port
   B When it's about to stop
   C When it's about to do a 360° turn

4 What is the European architectural style Romanesque called in Britain?

   A Classical Baroque
   B Norman
   C Gothic

5 What film studio did Alfred Hitchcock make the first British 'talkie' in?

   A Ealing
   B Pinewood
   C Elstree

6 What queen has reigned longer than any other monarch in Britain?

   A Elizabeth I
   B Victoria
   C Elizabeth II

7 In archery competition, what does the jargon term a 'Robin Hood' describe?

   A A competitor who plays in lincoln green
   B A shot driven into an arrow already in the target
   C An outstanding competitor

8 How many sides has a heptagon?

   A 7
   B 8
   C 9

9 Where was the first British colony in America?

   A Virginia
   B Massachusetts
   C The Carolinas

10 What did the 1829 Emancipation Act let Catholics do?

   A Become MPs
   B Vote
   C Worship

11 What illness, as depicted in *The Madness of King George*, runs in the British royal family?

   A Porphyria
   B Haemophilia
   C Schizophrenia

12 Who is the patron saint of ecologists?

   A St Isidore the Farmer
   B St Francis
   C St Timothy

153

1 If you were travelling at Mach 1, what speed would you be doing?

    A The speed of sound
    B The full capacity of the machine you were flying
    C 1000 mph

2 How much would an old sixpence be worth in modern decimal currency?

    A 6 pence
    B 2½ pence
    C 10 pence

3 Bill Haley's *Rock Around The Clock* was the theme song for which film?

    A *The Girl Can't Help It*
    B *Rebel Without A Cause*
    C *The Blackboard Jungle*

4 Who were the first team to win the first-ever Football League in 1889?

    A Sunderland
    B Preston North End
    C Everton

5 What is the richest country in the world?

    A Luxembourg
    B Monaco
    C The USA

6 What duetting High Society pairing sang *Well, Did You Evah?*

    A Bob Hope and Bing Crosby
    B Grace Kelly and Bing Crosby
    C Frank Sinatra and Bing Crosby

7 Who devised the first ballpoint pen?

  A Baron Bic
  B Laszlo Bíró
  C Louis E. Waterman

8 Where were the Elgin Marbles originally taken from?

  A The Parthenon in Athens
  B Apollo's Temple at Delphi
  C Zeus's Temple at Olympia

9 What did Charing Cross in London originally mark?

  A A medieval crossroads and marketplace
  B The funeral procession route of Queen Eleanor
  C A good place to build a railway station

10 What group of people did Cromwell allow to re-enter the country in 1656?

  A The Catholics
  B The Irish
  C The Jews

11 From what film comes the line, 'They call me Mister Tibbs'?

  A In The Heat Of The Night
  B Home Of The Brave
  C Guess Who's Coming To Dinner

12 How many orders of angels were there traditionally thought to be?

  A 1
  B 9
  C 3

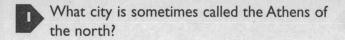

1 What city is sometimes called the Athens of the north?

    A Copenhagen
    B Edinburgh
    C Amsterdam

2 In heraldry, what colour would be described as gules?

    A Yellow
    B Green
    C Red

3 In the film *Speed*, what mph must the bus not drop below to avoid being blown up?

    A 50 mph
    B 55 mph
    C 58 mph

4 Income tax was first introduced in Britain to finance what war?

    A Boer War
    B Napoleonic Wars
    C The American War of 1812

5 Which of the following romantic film leads did Laurence Olivier *not* play?

    A Mr Darcy
    B Heathcliff
    C Mr Rochester

6 What do the letters DVD stand for?

    A Digital versatile disk
    B Digital video disk
    C Dodgy video duplicate

7 Who plays the character Begbie in the film *Trainspotting*?

   A Jonny Lee Miller
   B Robert Carlyle
   C Ewan McGregor

8 Which cricketer has scored most runs in any one test match innings?

   A Brian Lara
   B Matthew Hayden
   C Gary Sobers

9 What was Yuri Gagarin first to do?

   A First to orbit the earth
   B First in space
   C First to walk in space

10 Two of the Powerpuff Girls are Bubbles and Blossom; who is the third?

   A Buttercup
   B Baby
   C Bonnie

11 What country left the Commonwealth in 1949?

   A Ethiopia
   B India
   C Ireland

12 What song gave Tori Amos her first UK number one?

   A *Cornflake Girl*
   B *Pretty Good Year*
   C *Professional Widow*

1	A
2	B
3	C
4	B
5	A
6	C
7	B
8	A
9	B
10	C
11	A
12	B

1 What was the last number 1 hit single of the last millennium?

    A *She's The One* by Robbie Williams
    B *The Millennium Prayer* by Cliff Richard
    C *I Have A Dream/Seasons In The Sun* by Westlife

2 Why were 10 plagues visited on the ancient Egyptians?

    A They were not building Pyramids fast enough
    B They were unbelievers holding the Jews in slavery
    C As symbols of Egypt's future destruction

3 What is the name of Sindy doll's boyfriend?

    A Ken
    B Paul
    C Richard

4 In what year was the world's first telephone call made?

    A 1876
    B 1890
    C 1901

5 What musical features the song *New York, New York*?

    A *Wonderful Town*
    B *On The Town*
    C *Up In Central Park*

6 What was the first-ever feature-length animated film?

    A *Steamboat Willie*
    B *Fantasia*
    C *Snow White And The Seven Dwarfs*

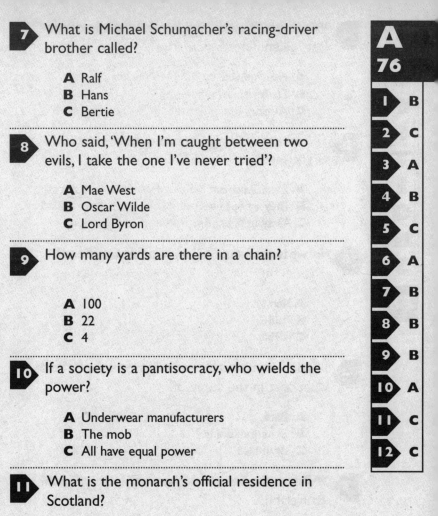

7 What is Michael Schumacher's racing-driver brother called?

    A Ralf
    B Hans
    C Bertie

8 Who said, 'When I'm caught between two evils, I take the one I've never tried'?

    A Mae West
    B Oscar Wilde
    C Lord Byron

9 How many yards are there in a chain?

    A 100
    B 22
    C 4

10 If a society is a pantisocracy, who wields the power?

    A Underwear manufacturers
    B The mob
    C All have equal power

11 What is the monarch's official residence in Scotland?

    A Balmoral
    B Edinburgh Castle
    C Palace of Holyroodhouse

12 What does the Welsh word 'Eisteddfod' actually mean?

    A Performance
    B Sitting
    C Music

A 76

1	B
2	C
3	A
4	B
5	C
6	A
7	B
8	B
9	B
10	A
11	C
12	C

1 In the 1920s, what did Prohibition outlaw in the USA?

   A Free speech
   B Drugs
   C Alcohol

2 Who is the youngest female artist ever to have a UK million-selling hit?

   A Lena Zavaroni
   B Britney Spears
   C Debbie Gibson

3 In what year did Halley's Comet last fly past the Earth?

   A 1996
   B 1986
   C 1990

4 If you were a batologist, what would you be a specialist in the study of?

   A Bats
   B Baits for fishing
   C Brambles

5 What is the second-largest city in the Republic of Ireland?

   A Galway
   B Cork
   C Limerick

6 What was the name of the pig in the Disney animation *Toy Story*?

   A Hamm
   B Mr Fats
   C Pig-boy

7 Who once declared, 'I started at the top and worked down'?

    A Orson Welles
    B Prince Charles
    C Wolfgang Amadeus Mozart

8 Who was the Scotland manager in the 1978 World Cup in Argentina?

    A Willie Ormond
    B Andy Roxburgh
    C Ally McLeod

9 What is Santa Clara county in California famous as?

    A The home of Hollywood
    B The home of Silicon Valley
    C The likely epicentre of the next big earthquake

10 Who was the only actor ever nominated for an Oscar for a *Star Wars* film?

    A Peter Cushing
    B Ian McDiarmid
    C Alec Guinness

11 What area did Frederick Delius make his name in?

    A Painting
    B Composing
    C Mathematics

12 What is Doggett's Coat and Badge?

    A An annual sculls race
    B An annual horse race
    C An annual greyhound race

1 Whose diary featured an eye-witness account of the Great Fire of London?

   A Jonathan Swift
   B Samuel Pepys
   C Sydney Smith

2 What US space programme put Americans into space for the first time?

   A Mercury
   B Apollo
   C Gemini

3 What year did British CD single sales first outsell all other singles formats combined?

   A 1990
   B 1993
   C 1996

4 If an Australian described something as bonzer, what would they mean?

   A Defective
   B Embarrassing
   C Excellent

5 What waterway links North America's Great Lakes with the Atlantic?

   A The Hudson River
   B The St Lawrence Seaway
   C The Panama Canal

6 What year was Concorde's maiden commercial flight?

   A 1972
   B 1974
   C 1976

7 'He gives her class and she gives him sex.' What couple was being described here?

 A Fred Astaire and Ginger Rogers
 B Prince Charles and Camilla Parker-Bowles
 C Hugh Grant and Liz Hurley

8 What road had Paul been travelling on when he experienced his conversion to Christianity?

 A The road to Damascus
 B The road to Jerusalem
 C The road to Nazareth

9 What is golfer Tiger Woods' real first name?

 A Caleb
 B Eldrick
 C Timothy

10 What king was known as the Merry Monarch?

 A Edward VII
 B Henry VIII
 C Charles II

11 What 007 took a lead role in the supernatural Disney classic *Darby O'Gill and the Little People*?

 A Pierce Brosnan
 B Roger Moore
 C Sean Connery

12 What British innovator founded the Habitat chain of shops?

 A Norman Foster
 B Terence Conran
 C Richard Rogers

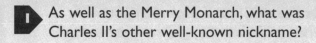

1 As well as the Merry Monarch, what was Charles II's other well-known nickname?

  A Old Roger
  B Old Rowley
  C Old Rogue

2 What sport did Evonne Goolagong become famous in?

  A Tennis
  B Running
  C Swimming

3 What countries are separated by the 38th parallel?

  A Canada and the USA
  B North and South Korea
  C The USA and Mexico

4 Who was the leader of Malawi for 30 years from its independence?

  A Hastings Banda
  B Seretse Khama
  C Robert Mugabe

5 In what year did underground trains first operate in London?

  A 1863
  B 1875
  C 1882

6 How many years must whisky mature before it can be called whisky?

  A 3
  B 5
  C 7

7 What country is the second-largest music market in the world?

    A UK
    B Japan
    C Australia

8 What is the world's largest mammal?

    A Killer whale
    B Blue whale
    C African elephant

9 What might you expect someone to do with a shillelagh?

    A Dance over it
    B Keep it as a weapon
    C Use it to summon leprechauns

10 In *The Wizard Of Oz*, what did Dorothy have to say to get back home to Kansas?

    A I want to get back to Kansas
    B There's no place like home
    C Ding, dong, the wicked witch is dead

11 Who masterminded the disastrous World War I attack on Gallipoli in 1915?

    A Field Marshal Haig
    B Prime Minister Asquith
    C First Lord of the Admiralty Winston Churchill

12 Where does the partner of London's Cleopatra's Needle stand?

    A Alexandria in Egypt
    B Paris
    C New York

A
79

1	B
2	A
3	C
4	C
5	B
6	C
7	A
8	A
9	B
10	C
11	C
12	B

1 Three Britons have won the Olympic men's 100 metres: Allan Wells, Linford Christie ... and who?

    A Eric Liddell
    B Harold Abrahams
    C Henry Stallard

2 What record does the three-toed sloth hold?

    A It is the only three-toed mammal
    B It is the slowest mammal in the world
    C It is the highest jumper, reaching heights of 18 ft

3 What was World War I flying ace Manfred von Richthofen better known as?

    A The Flying Frankfurter
    B The Red Baron
    C The German Devil

4 Who was king after Edward VIII?

    A William IV
    B George VI
    C Henry VII

5 Where in an American car would you store your luggage?

    A In the hood
    B In the trunk
    C In the fender

6 What musical and film featured a Nazi rallying song, *Tomorrow Belongs To Me*?

    A *Little Shop of Horrors*
    B *Cabaret*
    C *They're Playing Our Song*

7 Los Del Mar and Los Del Rio both had hits in 1996 with one song; what was it?

   A *No Tengo Dinero*
   B *La Bamba*
   C *Macarena*

8 How many political parties were allowed when Spain was ruled by General Franco?

   A One
   B Two
   C As many as people wanted

9 Where do the Chelsea Pensioners live?

   A Chelsea
   B Aldershot
   C Dartmouth

10 What does it mean for an MP to apply for stewardship of the Chiltern Hundreds?

   A The MP is seeking higher office
   B The MP is being demoted
   C The MP is resigning

11 In what classic 30s gangster film were James Cagney's last words, 'Made it Ma, top of the world'?

   A *White Heat*
   B *The Public Enemy*
   C *The Roaring Twenties*

12 What king from ancient Greek mythology turned everything he touched into gold?

   A Agamemnon
   B Solomon
   C Midas

A
80

1 B
2 A
3 B
4 A
5 A
6 A
7 B
8 B
9 B
10 B
11 C
12 C

167

1 Thomas Edison said genius was part inspiration, part perspiration; what were the proportions?

   A 1% inspiration and 99% perspiration
   B 100% inspiration and 0% perspiration
   C 50% inspiration and 50% perspiration

2 What singer is Marvin Lee Aday better known as?

   A Billy Ocean
   B Meatloaf
   C Method Man

3 What film was advertised with the caption, 'Growing! Growing! Growing! When will it stop'?

   A *King Kong*
   B *The Amazing Colossal Man*
   C *Frankenstein*

4 What language did Jesus Christ speak?

   A Hebrew
   B Aramaic
   C Yiddish

5 What contender has won most golds in any one Olympics?

   A Mark Spitz (swimming)
   B Nadia Comaneci (gymnastics)
   C Raymond Ewry (track & field)

6 'Give me your tired, your poor/Your huddled masses yearning to breathe free.' Where is this written?

   A On a plaque where the Bastille Prison stood
   B On the base of the Statue of Liberty
   C Over the door of the Customs offices at Dover

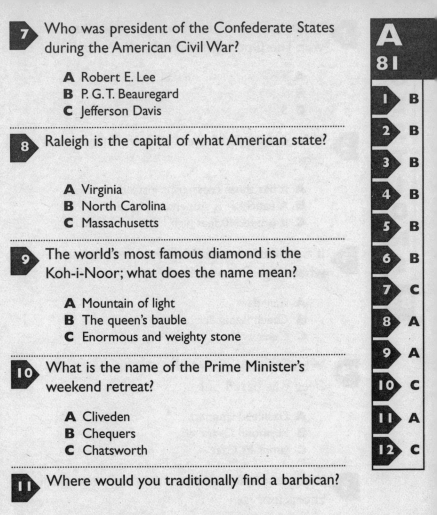

7 Who was president of the Confederate States during the American Civil War?

- **A** Robert E. Lee
- **B** P. G. T. Beauregard
- **C** Jefferson Davis

8 Raleigh is the capital of what American state?

- **A** Virginia
- **B** North Carolina
- **C** Massachusetts

9 The world's most famous diamond is the Koh-i-Noor; what does the name mean?

- **A** Mountain of light
- **B** The queen's bauble
- **C** Enormous and weighty stone

10 What is the name of the Prime Minister's weekend retreat?

- **A** Cliveden
- **B** Chequers
- **C** Chatsworth

11 Where would you traditionally find a barbican?

- **A** Guarding the entrance to a castle
- **B** Being used as a Crusader's weapon
- **C** Housing precious books in a medieval monastery

12 What was Gandhi's first name?

- **A** Mahatma
- **B** Mohammed
- **C** Mohandas

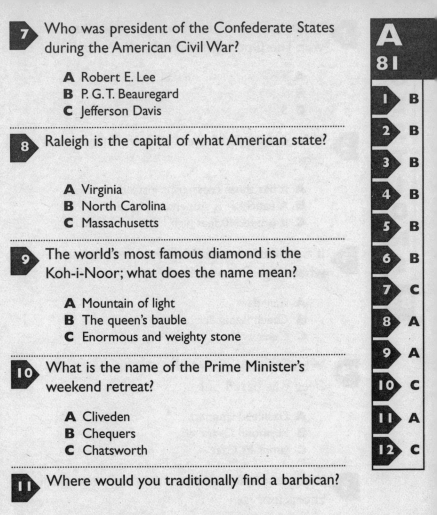

A 81

1	B
2	B
3	B
4	B
5	B
6	B
7	C
8	A
9	A
10	C
11	A
12	C

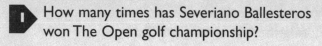
1 How many times has Severiano Ballesteros won The Open golf championship?

    A 1
    B 2
    C 3

2 How does a papal cross differ from a normal cross?

    A It has three cross-arms instead of one
    B A papal hat is suspended above it
    C It is over 10 feet high

3 If a car carries a nationality badge reading C, where does it come from?

    A Canada
    B Czech Republic
    C Cuba

4 Who wrote the book that the movie *The Big Sleep* was based on?

    A Dashiell Hammett
    B Raymond Chandler
    C James M. Cain

5 What major British town did the Romans call Eboracum?

    A Edinburgh
    B York
    C Ipswich

6 Who played Obi Wan Kenobi in the original *Star Wars* film?

    A Alec Guinness
    B Peter Cushing
    C Ewan McGregor

7 What is the middle name of recent US President Bill Clinton?

  A Kennedy
  B Jefferson
  C Washington

8 With what British singer did Ryuichi Sakamoto collaborate on his 1983 hit *Forbidden Colours*?

  A David Bowie
  B David Sylvian
  C David Gahan

9 Which of her residences did Queen Victoria die in?

  A Balmoral
  B Windsor Castle
  C Osborne House

10 What lies at the inner core of the Earth?

  A Solid iron
  B An oxygen and silicon compound
  C Liquid fire

11 What country is the port of Antwerp in?

  A Netherlands
  B Belgium
  C Germany

12 What time was it when the mouse ran up the clock?

  A 12 o'clock
  B 1 o'clock
  C 3 o'clock

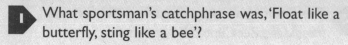

1 What sportsman's catchphrase was, 'Float like a butterfly, sting like a bee'?

  A Diego Maradona
  B Muhammad Ali
  C Will Carling

2 If you had a firkin of beer, how much beer would you have?

  A 6 pints
  B 2¹/2 gallon
  C 9 gallons

3 What Scots band sent a *Letter From America* in 1987?

  A Del Amitri
  B The Proclaimers
  C Deacon Blue

4 How long is the Channel Tunnel (to the nearest mile)?

  A 32
  B 37
  C 41

5 What is unusual about the doctor in the film *Star Trek: Voyager*?

  A He is an android
  B He is a Borg
  C He is a hologram

6 When was the £2 coin first introduced into Britain?

  A 1997
  B 1998
  C 1999

7 The Berlin Wall came down in 1989; how long (to the nearest year) did it stand?

    A 44 years
    B 29 years
    C 36 years

8 What were the names of the three novelist Brontë sisters?

    A Charlotte, Emily and Anne
    B Charlotte, Emily and Branwell
    C Charlotte, Emily and Jane

9 What is a glee club?

    A A choral-music singing society
    B A stand-up comedy club
    C A society where members buy and exchange gifts

10 In what film did Robert Shaw play Captain Quint?

    A *Moby Dick*
    B *Jaws*
    C *The Poseidon Adventure*

11 Where does the word 'navvy' derive from?

    A It was an old slang term for unskilled labouring
    B From 'Navy', as many ex-sailors became labourers
    C It was short for 'navigator' or canal builder

12 What motorway links Glasgow and Edinburgh?

    A M6
    B M8
    C M9

1   C
2   A
3   C
4   B
5   B
6   A
7   B
8   B
9   C
10   A
11   B
12   B

1 Why was it said that buttons were added to the cuffs of British Army uniforms in the 19th century?

   A So soldiers could see each other more easily
   B So they would look smart
   C So they wouldn't wipe their noses on their sleeves

2 On the Mohs scale of minerals, what is distinctive about talc?

   A It can be blown away
   B It is the only one sold commercially
   C It is at the bottom of the scale of hardness

3 What happened to Pharaoh's army as they chased the Israelites fleeing Egypt?

   A They were drowned in the Red Sea
   B They got lost in the sand dunes
   C The Israelites turned and slew them

4 What film had Holly Golightly as its main character?

   A *Guys And Dolls*
   B *Breakfast At Tiffany's*
   C *Singin' In The Rain*

5 What country was invaded by Mussolini's Italian forces in 1939?

   A Abyssinia
   B Albania
   C Austria

6 What is the world's largest diamond?

   A The Koh-i-Noor
   B Welcome Stranger
   C Cullinan

7 What famous artist plays drums with the group *Fat Les*?

    A Damien Hirst
    B David Hockney
    C Peter Howson

8 What is the name Glomma given to?

    A A ball of flying spittle
    B A blood vessel
    C A river in Norway

9 Which Beatle was first to have a solo number 1 hit?

    A George Harrison
    B John Lennon
    C Paul McCartney

10 What do a Brimstone, a Large Blue and a Painted Lady have in common?

    A They are pottery shapes
    B They are butterflies
    C They are famous paintings

11 What slasher movie introduced razor-fingered Freddie Krueger?

    A *Halloween*
    B *Nightmare On Elm Street*
    C *Friday The 13th*

12 Verdi wrote three operas based on Shakespeare's plays: *Macbeth, Otello* … and what?

    A *Roméo Et Juliette*
    B *Troilus And Cressida*
    C *Falstaff*

A
84

1 **B**
2 **C**
3 **B**
4 **A**
5 **C**
6 **B**
7 **B**
8 **A**
9 **A**
10 **B**
11 **C**
12 **B**

1 What is the most common element in the Universe?

A Oxygen
B Hydrogen
C Nitrogen

2 Where is the New England Range of mountains?

A USA
B Australia
C New Zealand

3 In what century was the first recorded trial by jury in England?

A 11th century
B 13th century
C 14th century

4 Who was the first member of the *EastEnders* cast to have a top 10 hit?

A Nick Berry
B Wendy Richards
C Anita Dobson

5 What is a Gloucester Old Spot?

A A variety of pig
B A wildflower local to the southwest
C An ale

6 What was the first movie ever to feature a vampire?

A *Dracula*
B *Nosferatu*
C *Vampyr*

7 Who as a baby was set afloat in a basket on the River Nile?

    A Tutankhamun
    B Moses
    C Cleopatra

8 What royal English house was represented by a white rose?

    A York
    B Lancaster
    C Tudor

9 What was the area where Calvary was also known as?

    A Gethsemane
    B Gennesaret
    C Golgotha

10 Who was described as being 'Mad, bad and dangerous to know'?

    A Lord Byron
    B Lord Alfred Douglas
    C Jim Morrison

11 What was the 18th-century figure Capability Brown famous for?

    A Saving the king in an assassination attempt
    B His rich tenor singing voice
    C Landscape gardening and design

12 Who was the Liberal leader in the party's landslide general election victory of 1906?

    A David Lloyd George
    B William Ewart Gladstone
    C Henry Campbell-Bannerman

1 What singer is footballer Jamie Redknapp married to?

A Baby Spice
B Louise Nurding
C Nicole Appleton

2 If someone has a fear of God, what are they said to suffer from?

A Theophobia
B Godophobia
C Deiophobia

3 What company issued the first-ever general credit card?

A American Express
B Barclays Bank
C Diners Club

4 What does a deltiologist collect?

A Stamps
B Postcards
C Phone cards

5 What film ends with the line, 'Nah, I'd only blow it'?

A *Get Carter*
B *The Sting*
C *The Third Man*

6 How did the colonists disguise to get on board British ships during the Boston Tea Party?

A They dressed as British sailors
B They dressed as Native American Indians
C They dressed as sacks of tea

7 'Reality hasn't really intervened in my mother's life since the 70s.' Whose child said this?

    A The Queen's
    B Princess Diana's
    C Margaret Thatcher's

8 Which of the following is not a blood group?

    A AB
    B O
    C BO

9 What was the famous jazz club founded in New York's Harlem in 1923?

    A The Cotton Club
    B The Apollo
    C Ragtime Roll

10 What country ruled Palestine until 1918?

    A Turkey
    B Britain
    C Russia

11 How long did the World War II night-time bombing Blitz on London last?

    A 8 months
    B 18 months
    C 28 months

12 If it is 6 am on 22 July in Britain, what time is it by Greenwich Mean Time?

    A 5am
    B 6am
    C 7am

A
86

1 **B**
2 **B**
3 **A**
4 **B**
5 **A**
6 **B**
7 **B**
8 **A**
9 **C**
10 **A**
11 **C**
12 **C**

1 Who said, 'Tolerance is the virtue of the weak'?

A Ian Paisley
B Ayatollah Khomeini
C The Marquis de Sade

2 In what North American city is the Space Needle?

A Toronto
B Seattle
C Vancouver

3 What is the badge of rank of a British Army corporal?

A One stripe
B Two stripes
C Three stripes

4 What film features Al Pacino as a bisexual bank robber?

A *Scarface*
B *Dog Day Afternoon*
C *Dick Tracy*

5 What country has the longest-reigning royal family in Europe?

A Monaco
B Spain
C Netherlands

6 Where was the Titanic built?

A Glasgow
B Belfast
C Tyneside

7 How many fluid ounces are in a pint?

   A 14
   B 16
   C 20

8 Which was considered the most important of southern England's Cinque Ports?

   A Sandwich
   B Dover
   C Hastings

9 What was the charge for which Scottish patriot William Wallace was executed in London?

   A Defeating the English
   B Raiding the north of England
   C Treason

10 The Jordanaires were the backing band of what rock and roll legend?

   A Elvis Presley
   B Little Richard
   C Bill Haley

11 What fanatical French revolutionary leader was known as the Sea-Green Incorruptible?

   A Robespierre
   B Danton
   C Marat

12 In what decade did France officially abolish the guillotine?

   A 1980s
   B 1960s
   C 1950s

A
87

1 B
2 A
3 C
4 B
5 B
6 B
7 C
8 C
9 A
10 A
11 A
12 A

1 What dolly did Aqua sing about in 1997?

    A Barbie
    B Sindy
    C Tiny Tears

2 What type of plant does the heart stimulant drug digitalis derive from?

    A Bluebell
    B Foxglove
    C Lavender

3 What musical featured the characters Maria and Tony as a latter-day *Romeo and Juliet*?

    A *West Side Story*
    B *Stop The World, I Want To Get Off*
    C *She Loves Me*

4 What empire gained the nickname 'the sick man of Europe' in the 19th century?

    A Austro-Hungarian
    B Ottoman
    C Russian

5 What was Peter Stuyvesant famed for in America?

    A Founding a cigarette company
    B Governing New Amsterdam
    C Captaining the Mayflower

6 Who was the American presidential retreat Camp David named after?

    A President Eisenhower
    B President Eisenhower's father
    C President Eisenhower's grandson

7 How many revolutions were there in Russia in 1917?

    A 1
    B 2
    C 4

8 What jazz musician's nickname was Yardbird?

    A Charlie Parker
    B Louis Armstrong
    C Billy Strayhorn

9 What is the only sequel ever to have lifted the Best Picture Oscar?

    A *The Empire Strikes Back*
    B *The Godfather Part II*
    C *Rocky II*

10 If you performed a mambo, what would you be doing?

    A Performing a voodoo ritual
    B Dancing
    C Playing music

11 What is Britain's highest military award for bravery?

    A CDM
    B Silver Star
    C Victoria Cross

12 After 7, what is the next prime number up?

    A 9
    B 11
    C 13

A
88

1	C
2	B
3	B
4	B
5	A
6	B
7	C
8	C
9	C
10	A
11	A
12	A

1 Whose last words were reported to have been, 'Be British'?

   A Nelson
   B Captain Scott
   C The Captain of the Titanic

2 What type of fruit is ananas?

   A Mango
   B Banana
   C Pineapple

3 What was the German codename for their invasion of the Soviet Union in 1941?

   A Barbarossa
   B Attila
   C Napoleon

4 Who directed *Back to the Future* and *Forrest Gump*?

   A Steven Spielberg
   B Lawrence Kasdan
   C Robert Zemeckis

5 Who passed as Betty Burke on a sail from Benbecula to Portree?

   A Prince Charles, the Prince of Wales, in a prank
   B Charles II fleeing Cromwell's troops
   C Bonnie Prince Charlie fleeing after Culloden

6 What city did *King Kong* terrorise?

   A Hong Kong
   B New York
   C Chicago

7 How many litres of air does a fit, healthy adult inhale with each breath?

    A 1
    B 2
    C 4

8 How many species of bat are there in Britain?

    A 8
    B 16
    C 28

9 What century did the Saxons first settle in England?

    A Fourth
    B Fifth
    C Sixth

10 What film featured the 1976 Starland Vocal Band hit *Afternoon Delight*?

    A *Good Will Hunting*
    B *The Dead Poets Society*
    C *Dogma*

11 If music is to be played pianissimo, how should it be played?

    A Very loudly
    B Very softly
    C With sudden force

12 What Midwestern US state is the city of Des Moines in?

    A Nebraska
    B Iowa
    C Wisconsin

A
89

1   **A**
2   **B**
3   **A**
4   **B**
5   **B**
6   **C**
7   **B**
8   **A**
9   **B**
10   **B**
11   **C**
12   **B**

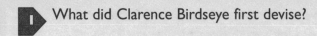

Q U E S T I O N S 91

1 What did Clarence Birdseye first devise?

  A Fish fingers
  B A workable way to freeze food
  C Cardboard packaging that stayed rigid in a freezer

2 What stretched 2000 miles from Independence, Missouri, to the Columbia River in the west?

  A The Snake River
  B The Sioux Homeland
  C The Oregon Trail

3 In the early 80s, who was the Dandy Highwayman?

  A Malcolm McLaren
  B Simon le Bon
  C Adam Ant

4 What was a knight errant?

  A A knight wandering in search of chivalrous deeds
  B A knight doing penance for past mistakes
  C A knight attached to a particular ruler or castle

5 If you sold your bonham in Ireland, what would you have just done?

  A Sold a piglet
  B Given away all your money
  C Vowed to stop drinking

6 What was the name of the sheep successfully cloned by Edinburgh scientists in 1996?

  A Daisy
  B Dolly
  C Dizzy

186

7 Two of the three Magi, or Wise Men, were Melchior and Caspar; who was the third?

    A Balthazar
    B Beelzebub
    C Brian

8 What West Indian flag features three over-lapping triangles in its centre?

    A Barbados
    B St Lucia
    C Montserrat

9 In what film did John Travolta play Danny Zucco?

    A *Saturday Night Fever*
    B *Grease*
    C *Pulp Fiction*

10 What were Nazi Germany's Geheime Staatspolizei better known as?

    A The Waffen-SS
    B The Wehrmacht
    C The Gestapo

11 What happened to the original glass-and-metal Alexandra Palace?

    A It burned down
    B It fell down
    C It was closed down

12 What are Tup's Indispensable, Furnace Dapping and Green Highlander?

    A Scottish reels
    B Embroidery stitches
    C Fishing flies

A 90

1	C
2	C
3	A
4	C
5	C
6	B
7	C
8	B
9	B
10	A
11	B
12	B

1 How many times was Austrian driver Niki Lauda World Formula One champion?

A 3
B 4
C 5

2 What does a beta-blocker block?

A Hormone-releasing nervous activity
B Stimulating excess blood flow
C Movement of free radicals through the body

3 In the NATO alphabet, what word is given to represent the letter Q?

A Quick
B Queen
C Quebec

4 Where did the first European land in Australia?

A Bondi Beach
B Botany Bay
C Van Diemen's Land

5 What film opens with the words, 'I believe in America'?

A *How The West Was Won*
B *The Birth of A Nation*
C *The Godfather*

6 What two countries does the Brenner Pass link?

A Germany and Switzerland
B Italy and Switzerland
C Italy and Austria

7 What is Fatboy Slim's real name?

   A Norman Vaughan
   B Norman Cook
   C Norman Ball

8 Where is Disneyland?

   A Paris
   B Florida
   C California

9 In what year did driving licences become compulsory in Britain?

   A 1903
   B 1923
   C 1943

10 What song has the line 'And we'll all be lonely tonight and lonely tomorrow'?

   A *Nothing Ever Happens*
   B *Heaven Knows I'm Miserable Now*
   C *Don't Look Back In Anger*

11 What American football team is based in the Pennsylvania town of Pittsburgh?

   A Pittsburgh Lakers
   B Pittsburgh Steelers
   C Pittsburgh Patriots

12 How many eyes did the mythical creature Cyclops have?

   A 1
   B 2
   C 3

A
91

1 B
2 C
3 C
4 A
5 A
6 B
7 A
8 B
9 B
10 C
11 A
12 C

189

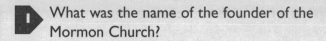
1 What was the name of the founder of the Mormon Church?

   A Joseph La Fayette
   B Joseph Smith
   C Joseph Mormon

2 What ship carried the Pilgrim Fathers to Massachusetts in 1620?

   A The Puritan
   B The God Speed
   C The Mayflower

3 What appears in the centre of the flag of Brazil?

   A A globe with Rio de Janiero at its centre
   B The stellar constellations as viewed from Rio
   C A football with Brazil in its centre

4 What 1980s film featured music from the opera *La Wally*?

   A *Diva*
   B *A Passage To India*
   C *Rocky III*

5 Who searched for revenge on the whale Moby Dick after it bit off his leg?

   A Ishmael
   B Queequeg
   C Captain Ahab

6 What brothers considered themselves on a mission from God?

   A The Blues Brothers
   B The Earp Brothers
   C The Wright Brothers

7 What writer's life and marriage were dramatised in *Shadowlands*?

   A H. G. Wells
   B T. S. Eliot
   C C. S. Lewis

8 What company made the first mass-produced car?

   A Oldsmobile
   B Ford
   C Triumph

9 Where might you expect to find a Japanese shogun?

   A Mounted on a wall
   B Tied defensively around the chest
   C Leading an army

10 What is the last letter of the ancient Greek alphabet?

   A Zeta
   B Omega
   C Upsilon

11 If you were suffering from a bleb, what would you expect it to be?

   A An intestinal worm
   B A blister
   C An abnormal growth on the tongue

12 Who has spent more weeks in the British charts than any other artist?

   A The Beatles
   B Elvis Presley
   C Madonna

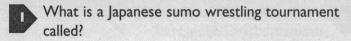

QUESTIONS

1 What is a Japanese sumo wrestling tournament called?

   A Biffo
   B Basho
   C Bonko

2 What was Edward VIII more commonly known as by his friends and family?

   A Eddie
   B Jim
   C David

3 Who once said of Wales, 'The land of my fathers. My fathers can have it'?

   A Prince Charles
   B Dylan Thomas
   C Catherine Zeta Jones

4 The classic *Top Of The Pops* theme is taken from a Led Zeppelin song. What is it?

   A *Whole Lotta Love*
   B *Rock and Roll*
   C *Stairway to Heaven*

5 How many goals against South Korea were disallowed in the 2002 World Cup?

   A Three
   B Five
   C Eleven

6 Who is the potions master at Hogwarts School of Witchcraft and Wizardry?

   A Professor Phial
   B Professor Snape
   C Professor Brewer

7 What was introduced in 1617 to curb the 'rude behaviour' of London's carters and draymen?

A Large sticks were dispensed to all shopkeepers
B A one-way street was introduced
C Swear boxes were erected every 200 yards

8 Who composed the *Unfinished Symphony*?

A Schubert
B Schumann
C Brahms

9 What band recorded the 90s classic single *Common People*?

A Blur
B Pulp
C Manics

10 What would a Scotsman expect to find when confronted with Partan Bree?

A A traditional Highland eightsome reel
B A bowl of crab soup
C A bonnet with tassels instead of a pom-pom

11 What is the name of the werewolf in the *Buffy The Vampire Slayer* series?

A Oz
B Remus
C Lon

12 Which medieval fortress and prison did French revolutionaries storm on 14 July 1789?

A Versailles
B The Louvre
C The Bastille

A
93

1 B
2 C
3 B
4 A
5 C
6 A
7 C
8 A
9 C
10 B
11 B
12 B

193

1 Who in the Bible was turned into a pillar of salt?

    A King Herod
    B Lot's wife
    C The people of Sodom

2 Which ships fly the Red Ensign?

    A The centre ships in a war fleet
    B The mercantile marine
    C Royal Navy ships in peace time

3 In which year was the architect Sir Christopher Wren born?

    A 1612
    B 1622
    C 1632

4 Musician Declan McManus is better known as what?

    A Bob Geldof
    B Shane McGowan
    C Elvis Costello

5 From what did policemen get the nickname 'bobbies'?

    A Their peculiar gait on London's uneven streets
    B It was the nickname for a shilling, their annual pay
    C The first name of their founder was 'Robert'

6 What was the name of the dwarf member of the *Fellowship of the Ring*?

    A Legolas
    B Pippin
    C Gimli

7 What colour was the first aircraft Black Box?

  A Red
  B White
  C Black

8 How many squares are there on a chess board?

  A 49
  B 64
  C 72

9 What does Picasso's famous painting *Guernica* depict?

  A The aftermath of an earthquake in the 1920s
  B The bombing of the town during the Civil War
  C Local fans' frustration at their team's defeat

10 Who defined democracy as 'government of the people, by the people, for the people'?

  A Fidel Castro
  B Abraham Lincoln
  C Margaret Thatcher

11 In Alfred Hitchcock's *Rear Window*, why is James Stewart confined to his apartment?

  A He has broken his leg
  B He has been locked in
  C He has barricaded himself in

12 If you were chatting online, how would something hilarious make you feel?

  A GTG
  B PMFJI
  C ROTFL

1 In the R.L. Stevenson classic *Treasure Island*, what is the dreaded Black Spot?

    A The toilet on board a pirate ship
    B A notice of impending death
    C A nasty form of scurvy contracted by seafarers

2 Scientist Jonas Salk produced a life-saving virus in 1952. Which disease did it protect against?

    A Smallpox
    B Measles
    C Polio

3 Who wrote the scripts for the films *A Private Function* and *Prick Up Your Ears*?

    A Alan Ayckbourn
    B Alan Bennett
    C Alan Bleasdale

4 Which region does St Nicholas, the martyr behind the Father Christmas myth, come from?

    A Eastern Europe
    B The British Isles
    C Asia Minor

5 Which country is the world's largest oil producer?

    A The USA
    B Saudi Arabia
    C Venezuela

6 Who were the master-and-servant sketch duo from *The Fast Show*?

    A Ralph & Bob
    B Ted & Ralph
    C Bill & Ted

7 'Nintendo' is a Japanese word. What does it mean?

    A Leave luck to heaven
    B Fun television game
    C Too much excitement

8 Who were Balthazar, Melchior and Caspar?

    A Cartoon series ghosts
    B The Three Wise Men
    C Characters from US TV show *Saturday Night Live*

9 Who was the historical figure Salazar?

    A A Muslim leader against the Crusaders
    B A Portuguese right-wing dictator
    C A powerful Arab court conjurer and sorcerer

10 Who scored England's first goal in the 2002 World Cup finals?

    A David Beckham
    B Sol Campbell
    C Michael Owen

11 What was the Manics' first no. 1 hit in the UK?

    A *Design For Life*
    B *If You Tolerate This Your Children Will Be Next*
    C *Everything Must Go*

12 'The most gigantic ... futile and bloody fight ever ...' Who said this of the 1916 Battle of the Somme?

    A War Minister Lloyd George
    B Commander-in-Chief Douglas Haig
    C War poet Wilfred Owen

A 95

1	B
2	B
3	C
4	C
5	C
6	C
7	A
8	B
9	B
10	B
11	A
12	C

1 What was the Manics' hit *If You Tolerate This Your Children Will Be Next*, about?

   A The decline of the NHS
   B The Spanish Civil War
   C The state of the Wales national side

2 When was Monopoly invented?

   A 1936
   B 1926
   C 1946

3 Which was the only year Wales qualified for the World Cup finals?

   A 1954
   B 1958
   C 1972

4 What type of creatures were dinosaurs?

   A Reptiles
   B Rodents
   C Aves

5 Who said, 'Saints should always be judged guilty until they are proved innocent'?

   A George Orwell
   B Christopher Hitchens
   C Oscar Wilde

6 What is a gardener's main problem with growing mint?

   A It smells very strong
   B It spreads rapidly
   C It attracts cats

7 When did the toy My Little Pony first go on sale?

  A 1979
  B 1982
  C 1985

8 How many times has someone called 'James' been King of Scots?

  A Two
  B Seven
  C Nineteen

9 In what types of food is cholesterol found?

  A Food of animal origin only
  B Food of plant origin only
  C Any type of food

10 From what did the word 'Easter' originate?

  A A Celtic god who hunted each Beltane
  B The Saxon goddess of spring
  C A Byzantine god crucified by his people

11 How many times has Brazil won the World Cup?

  A Five
  B Four
  C Three

12 What is the name for the illusory pattern seen when curved parallel or periodic lines are superimposed?

  A Moiré
  B Sotto in sù
  C Trompe l'oeil

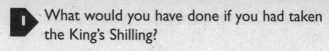

Q U E S T I O N S

98

1 What would you have done if you had taken the King's Shilling?

A Joined the Navy
B Joined the Army
C Stolen a pensioner's Maundy Money

2 In the hit TV series *The Sopranos*, what are Tony's children called?

A AJ and Meadow
B Christopher and Carmela
C Anthony and Livia

3 Who were runners up in the 2002 World Cup?

A South Korea
B Turkey
C Germany

4 In Roman numerals, how would you express the number 2003?

A MCIII
B MMIII
C MDIII

5 Who were the mythical warrior maidens who carried off fallen Viking heroes to Valhalla?

A Amazons
B Valkyries
C Dahomites

6 On what date does the feast of St Nicholas traditionally fall?

A 6th December
B 25th December
C 6th January

7 Why did Cat Stevens abandon his pop career?

    A Nobody was buying his records any more
    B He decided to go into producing
    C He became a Muslim

8 Where is a dog's height measured from?

    A The top of its head
    B Its rump
    C Its withers (behind its neck)

9 What king's nickname was 'The Bastard'?

    A Edward VII
    B Henry VIII
    C William I (the Conqueror)

10 What was listed in William the Conqueror's Domesday Book?

    A The number of souls in every parish in England
    B All lands and estates, and who held them
    C Barons who were suspected enemies of the king

11 What is unusual about the flag of Nepal?

    A It is not rectangular
    B It is completely grey
    C It has the words 'Visit Nepal' along the bottom

12 Which book does the Cheshire Cat appear in?

    A *The Wind In The Willows*
    B *Alice's Adventures In Wonderland*
    C *The Water Babies*

A
97

1 B
2 A
3 B
4 A
5 A
6 B
7 B
8 B
9 A
10 B
11 A
12 A

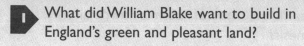
1 What did William Blake want to build in England's green and pleasant land?

    A A better world
    B Jerusalem
    C Britannia

2 The national car registration letters 'GBG' represent which country?

    A Guernsey
    B Gibraltar
    C Grenada

3 Which 20th-century US film star is named on the Warren Zevon hit, *Werewolves of London*?

    A Bela Lugosi
    B Boris Karloff
    C Lon Chaney

4 What 41-year-old is the oldest goalkeeper to play in the World Cup finals?

    A Pat Jennings
    B Gordon Banks
    C Dino Zoff

5 In bookmaker's slang, how much is a monkey?

    A £50
    B £500
    C £5000

6 Who were Ian Dury's backing group?

    A The Rhythm Sticks
    B The Blockheads
    C The Alberts

7 What is the name of Artemis Fowl's fairy nemesis?

   A Holly Short
   B Brenda Small
   C Tinkerbell Tiny

8 Terry Collier was one of the *Likely Lads*; who was the other?

   A Bob Richards
   B Bob Ferris
   C Bob Jones

9 According to writer Aldous Huxley, real orgies were never so exciting as what?

   A Pornographic books
   B A good fry-up
   C Pay day

10 In which sport would you attempt to get stones into a house?

   A Lacrosse
   B Curling
   C Croquet

11 In Greek mythology, which three-headed dog guarded the entrance to the Underworld?

   A Fluffy
   B Tricaput
   C Cerberus

12 What word represents the letter 'R' in the Nato alphabet?

   A Roger
   B Rickshaw
   C Romeo

A
98

1 B
2 A
3 C
4 B
5 B
6 A
7 C
8 C
9 C
10 B
11 A
12 B

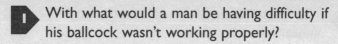

1 With what would a man be having difficulty if his ballcock wasn't working properly?

A His car engine
B His bodily processes
C His toilet

2 Along with Wat Tyler and John Ball, who was the main leader of the 1381 Peasants' Revolt?

A Jack Straw
B John Prescott
C Robin Cook

3 Which member of Bruce Springsteen's E Street Band has a starring role in TV's *The Sopranos*?

A Steven Van Zandt
B Danny Federici
C Patti Scialfa

4 If somebody Scottish has a ferntickle what do they have?

A A freckle
B A nettle rash
C A frog in their throat

5 Where were the Commonwealth Games held in 1998?

A Kuala Lumpur
B Edinburgh
C Sydney

6 What language is the source of the English art-related words 'easel', 'sketch' and 'landscape'?

A French
B German
C Dutch

7 The Portuguese dictator Salazar died in 1970. What caused his death?

    A A piece of shellfish lodged in his throat
    B A bite on the toe from a poisonous snake
    C Injuries suffered after his deck-chair collapsed

8 In the original comic, how did Peter Parker become Spiderman?

    A He was bitten by a radioactive spider
    B He was implanted with a spider gene
    C He contracted the rare jungle disease arachnaria

9 In what 1980s US TV show did B.A. Baracus feature?

    A *The Dukes of Hazzard*
    B *Knight Rider*
    C *The A Team*

10 What would you do if you took an emetic?

    A Vomit
    B Have diarrhoea
    C Stop having a fit

11 The Triathlon is comprised of three sports. Cycling and running are two; what is the third?

    A Jumping
    B Swimming
    C Archery

12 Who played Velma in the 2002 movie *Scooby Doo*?

    A Sarah Michelle Gellar
    B Linda Cardellini
    C Barbera Joseph

A
99

1	B
2	A
3	C
4	A
5	B
6	B
7	A
8	B
9	A
10	B
11	C
12	C

1 Which London band sings *Woke Up This Morning*, the theme music to TV's *The Sopranos*?

   A Bush
   B Alabama 3
   C E17

2 What name is given to the severe tropical cyclones of the Pacific Ocean?

   A Typhoon
   B Hurricane
   C Tsunami

3 If a vessel were flying a square blue-and-white chequered flag, what would that mean?

   A Keep clear I am manoeuvring with difficulty
   B I am dragging my anchor
   C No

4 What colour of uniforms do starfleet captains wear in *Star Trek: The Next Generation*?

   A Red
   B Blue
   C Mustard

5 In the New Testament, who was Barabas?

   A One of the thieves crucified with Jesus
   B The thief Pontius Pilate released instead of Jesus
   C The man who offered to carry the cross for Jesus

6 How many players in total take part in a normal rugby scrum?

   A 16
   B 20
   C As many as want to join in

7 Which of these countries has the lowest population density?

    A Australia
    B Canada
    C Iceland

8 How many gold medals did Britain win at the 2002 Winter Olympics?

    A None
    B One
    C Two

9 What is Austin Powers' job when he is not being an International Man of Mystery?

    A Fashion photographer
    B Newspaper reporter
    C Civil servant

10 If a dish is called 'florentine', what is it cooked with?

    A Cheese
    B Spinach
    C Eggs

11 Which MP first discovered the law of gravity?

    A Robert Boyle
    B John Pym
    C Isaac Newton

12 What was the South Sea Bubble?

    A Australia's best-selling bubble-gum ever
    B An area of the Pacific where ships disappeared
    C An 18th-century stock-market crash

1	C
2	A
3	A
4	A
5	A
6	C
7	C
8	A
9	C
10	A
11	B
12	B

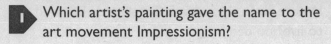

1 Which artist's painting gave the name to the art movement Impressionism?

    A Monet
    B Van Gogh
    C Dégas

2 Brass is made of two metals: one is copper, what is the other?

    A Nickel
    B Tin
    C Zinc

3 Which of the following mammals is the fastest?

    A Cat
    B Human
    C Elephant

4 What nationality was Prince Albert, Consort of Queen Victoria?

    A Greek
    B German
    C Austrian

5 In which African country is Timbuktu?

    A Sudan
    B Nigeria
    C Mali

6 Who wrote the sonnet which begins, 'How do I love thee? Let me count the ways'?

    A William Shakespeare
    B Lord Byron
    C Elizabeth Barrett Browning

7 Where were the ancient Greek gods believed to live?

    A Mount Olympus
    B The Parthenon
    C Delphi

8 Which Pulp song has the lyrics, 'But she didn't understand, She just smiled and held my hand'?

    A *Help The Aged*
    B *My Legendary Girlfriend*
    C *Common People*

9 Which Scot invented television?

    A Alexander Graham Bell
    B Andrew Carnegie
    C John Logie Baird

10 What is said to be the oldest university in the world?

    A Paris
    B Salamanca
    C Bologna

11 What is a widgeon?

    A A frothing gadget in a draught-beer can
    B A duck
    C A type of knot

12 What made Peru's goalkeeper Ramon Quiroga notable in the 1978 World Cup?

    A The tightness of his shorts
    B Scoring from a direct free kick in extra time
    C Being booked for a foul in the opposition half

A 101

1	B
2	A
3	C
4	A
5	B
6	A
7	A
8	B
9	A
10	B
11	C
12	C

1 Which of these novels is by John Fowles?

A *The English Patient*
B *The French Lieutenant's Woman*
C *The Tenant of Wildfell Hall*

2 Which country has the longest land border in the world?

A China
B Russia
C Brazil

3 The soundtrack to *Velvet Goldmine* features a cover of T Rex's *20th Century Boy*. Who sings it?

A Placebo
B Pulp
C Lou Reed

4 What were the eighteenth-century Hell-Fire Clubs devoted to?

A Abolishing religion
B Carriage-racing
C Debauchery

5 According to the First World War song, what was to be hung from the Siegfried Line?

A The Kaiser's underwear
B The German surrender
C The washing

6 What was Sir Thomas Raffles most famous for?

A Inventing the Gin and Tonic drink
B Founding Singapore
C Founding an upmarket hotel chain

7 If someone were born within the sound of Bow Bells, what would they be?

    A A limey
    B A cockney
    C Hard of hearing

8 Which part of the body does the disease scrofula, or the king's evil, affect?

    A The lymph glands
    B The nervous system
    C The genitals

9 According to the poem, what did Kubla Khan decree in Xanadu?

    A A stately pleasure dome
    B A noble marble throne
    C A gold and silver home

10 What is the Christian feast of Whitsun also known as?

    A Pentecost
    B Ascension Day
    C Palm Sunday

11 Who won the Golden Shoe in the 2002 World Cup?

    A Ronaldo
    B Rivaldo
    C Miroslav Klose

12 Who is the first character to speak in the original *Star Wars* film (Episode IV)?

    A C3PO
    B Darth Vader
    C Princess Leia

A 102

1 A
2 C
3 A
4 B
5 C
6 C
7 A
8 C
9 C
10 C
11 B
12 C

1 Which famous artist died during an outbreak of bubonic plague?

   A Rembrandt
   B Michelangelo
   C Titian

2 If you throw two dice, what number are you more likely to get than any other?

   A Ten
   B Seven
   C Four

3 What would a Scotsman do with his spurtle?

   A Put it in his sporran
   B Treasure it
   C Use it to stir his porridge

4 Six deadly sins are Anger, Avarice, Envy, Gluttony, Lust and Pride. What is the seventh?

   A Sloth
   B Bigotry
   C Poverty

5 In TV's *The Simpsons*, who is Mr Burns' assistant?

   A Waylon Skinner
   B Waylon Smithers
   C Waylon Simmonds

6 What country would a website be based in if the country domain were .cn?

   A Canada
   B China
   C Congo

7 *Under The Table And Dreaming* and *Everyday* are albums by which North American band?

    A REM
    B Dave Matthews Band
    C Barenaked Ladies

8 If it is 10 am in Anchorage, Alaska, what time is it in the UK?

    A 5 pm
    B 6 pm
    C 7 pm

9 Who did Alan Rickman play in the film *Dogma*?

    A Rufus, the thirteenth Apostle
    B God
    C Metatron

10 What historical figure gave Britain its name?

    A King Arthur
    B Brutus
    C Julius Caesar

11 What country came third in the 2002 World Cup?

    A Germany
    B Turkey
    C South Korea

12 When the Owl and the Pussycat went to sea, what did they take?

    A A small guitar
    B Some honey and plenty of money
    C A beautiful pea-green boat

A
103

1 **B**
2 **A**
3 **A**
4 **C**
5 **C**
6 **B**
7 **B**
8 **A**
9 **A**
10 **A**
11 **A**
12 **A**

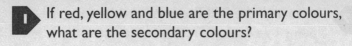
1 If red, yellow and blue are the primary colours, what are the secondary colours?

- **A** Green, purple and orange
- **B** Black and white
- **C** Pale red, pale yellow and pale blue

2 In the nursery rhyme, what did Solomon Grundy do on Friday?

- **A** Took ill
- **B** Was worse
- **C** Died

3 Who was the first man to successfully defend the 400m Olympic title?

- **A** Michael Johnson
- **B** Jon Drummond
- **C** Ato Boldon

4 What is Posh Spice's maiden name?

- **A** Victoria Beckham
- **B** Victoria Adams
- **C** Victoria Smith

5 Which American city produces Samuel Adams lager?

- **A** Milwaukee
- **B** Boston
- **C** Atlanta

6 Who created *The Magic Roundabout*?

- **A** Serge Danot
- **B** Eric Thompson
- **C** Oliver Postgate and Peter Firmin

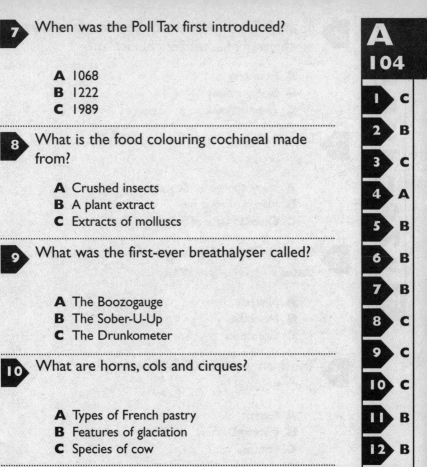

7 When was the Poll Tax first introduced?

    A 1068
    B 1222
    C 1989

8 What is the food colouring cochineal made from?

    A Crushed insects
    B A plant extract
    C Extracts of molluscs

9 What was the first-ever breathalyser called?

    A The Boozogauge
    B The Sober-U-Up
    C The Drunkometer

10 What are horns, cols and cirques?

    A Types of French pastry
    B Features of glaciation
    C Species of cow

11 What is a chasuble, and who would wear it?

    A It is a protective mask, worn by a riveter
    B It is a special belt, worn by a shepherd
    C It is an outer vestment, worn by a priest

12 Who is the lead singer of the band Limp Bizkit?

    A Fred Durst
    B John Otto
    C Sam Rivers

A

104

1	C
2	B
3	C
4	A
5	B
6	B
7	B
8	C
9	C
10	C
11	B
12	B

1 In which film did Johnny Depp play a detective on the trail of a headless horseman?

   A *From Hell*
   B *Sleepy Hollow*
   C *The Ninth Gate*

2 Who was known as Bloody Mary?

   A Mary, Queen of Scots
   B Mary I of England
   C Queen Maria of Spain

3 Carson City is the capital of which American state?

   A Nevada
   B Montana
   C Colorado

4 To which vegetable family does the coriander plant belong?

   A Carrot
   B Cabbage
   C Potato

5 Which type of creatures are the Canary Islands named after?

   A Canaries
   B Dogs
   C Parrots

6 What artist had most weeks in the UK chart in 2000?

   A Bob the Builder
   B Westlife
   C Craig David

7 What did Charlie Chaplin and Eva Peron have in common?

   A Both had a house in the Swiss Alps
   B Both were said to have been sexually insatiable
   C Both their bodies were stolen from their graves

8 Which mammal gestates its young for the longest period?

   A The African elephant
   B The white rhinoceros
   C The blue whale

9 Of whom did Jock Stein say, 'He knows what's happening 20 minutes before everybody else'?

   A Franz Beckenbauer
   B Alfredo Di Stéfano
   C Bobby Moore

10 Which of the following was not run as a British mandated territory after the First World War?

   A Egypt
   B Iraq
   C Palestine

11 What is the main component of Earth's atmosphere?

   A Oxygen
   B Nitrogen
   C Carbon dioxide

12 How many games are played in a rubber of bridge?

   A Three
   B Five
   C Nine

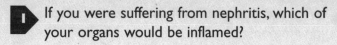

1 If you were suffering from nephritis, which of your organs would be inflamed?

A Liver
B Kidney
C Heart

2 What is said to have been the first major sports broadcast by satellite?

A Clay v Liston championship fight, Miami, 1964
B US Masters Golf Tournament, 1967
C England v West Germany World Cup Final, 1966

3 In Ireland, what is the Gaeltacht?

A The Gaelic Football League
B A movement promoting the use of Gaelic
C The Gaelic-speaking parts of Ireland

4 Hampden Park staged the European Cup finals in 1960 and 2002. What did they have in common?

A The final score was the same
B Real Madrid were the winners
C Fans in kilts and 'Jimmy' wigs invaded the pitch

5 The film character Patrick Bateman was said to have personified the 1980s. What was the film?

A *Wall Street*
B *The Firm*
C *American Psycho*

6 What is the world's longest mountain range?

A The Rockies
B The Andes
C The Himalayas

7 What was the name of Tam o' Shanter's horse?

   A Kate
   B Jean
   C Maggie

8 What colour is the gemstone lapis lazuli?

   A Blue
   B White
   C Silver

9 Who had a hit in 1990 with *Wicked Game*?

   A Chris Izaak
   B Deep Blue Something
   C Michael Bolton

10 According to legend, who was hidden inside the Trojan Horse?

   A Helen of Troy
   B Trojan soldiers
   C Greek soldiers

11 How many times did Damon Hill win the Formula 1 Drivers' World Championship?

   A Never
   B Once
   C Twice

12 Who called The Simpsons 'subtle propaganda in the cause of sense, humility and virtue'?

   A Rowan Williams, Archbishop of Canterbury
   B George W. Bush
   C David Beckham

1	B
2	B
3	A
4	A
5	B
6	C
7	C
8	A
9	C
10	A
11	B
12	A

1 Which British monarch was married to Mary of Teck?

   A George VI
   B Edward VII
   C George V

2 If a doctor wrote b.i.n. on a prescription, what would the patient be told to do?

   A Have the medication injected regularly
   B Throw the medication away after a period of time
   C Take the medication twice a night

3 In Chaucer's *Canterbury Tales*, the Wife of Bath's tale asks what women want most. What is it?

   A Love
   B Money
   C Freedom

4 Which country has the biggest proportion of its population in the army?

   A Israel
   B North Korea
   C Iraq

5 What 1991 Scorpions hit celebrated the fall of Communism in Russia?

   A *Wind of Change*
   B *Alien Nation*
   C *I've Got To Be Free*

6 Who were Thunderbirds' Tracy brothers Scott, Virgil, Alan, Gordon and John named after?

   A Gerry Anderson's friends
   B The first five US astronauts
   C Their puppets' respective makers

7 Which herb is used to flavour the tomato-based sauce on pizza?

    A Thyme
    B Rosemary
    C Oregano

8 Which organisation's newspaper is called *The War Cry*?

    A The Red Cross
    B The Boys' Brigade
    C The Salvation Army

9 In the motorcycling Isle of Man TT competition, what does TT stand for?

    A Tourist Trophy
    B Time Trial
    C Trials Trophy

10 What do presbyterians believe?

    A That souls are predestined to heaven or hell
    B That churches should be run without bishops
    C That the church's laws should control all society

11 How many players take the field in a Gaelic football team?

    A 13
    B 15
    C 12

12 In the 2002 World Cup England v Brazil match, which Brazilian lobbed Seaman from 40 yards?

    A Ronaldo
    B Rivaldo
    C Ronaldinho

A 107

1 B
2 A
3 C
4 B
5 C
6 B
7 C
8 A
9 A
10 C
11 B
12 A

221

1 What would you call painting so realistic it may fool viewers into thinking the objects are real?

   A Moiré
   B Sotto in sù
   C Trompe l'oeil

2 Which line on the London Underground map is represented in red?

   A District
   B Central
   C Circle

3 Where does the tomato plant originally come from?

   A China
   B India
   C South America

4 Which astrological symbol represents the period 23 November–22 December?

   A Sagittarius
   B Capricorn
   C Scorpio

5 What NFL team plays at the Arrowhead Stadium?

   A The Kansas City Chiefs
   B The Washington Redskins
   C The Buffalo Bills

6 Only one dwarf in Disney's Snow White did not have a beard. Which one?

   A Dopey
   B Happy
   C Grumpy

7 What was Wordsworth talking of when he said, 'Earth has not anything to show more fair'?

    A A host of golden daffodils
    B The lake at Grasmere
    C London

8 What is the highest rank in the British peerage?

    A Marquis
    B Earl
    C Duke

9 In computer technology, what does the 'R' in RAM stand for?

    A Random
    B Radio
    C Research

10 What is the main flavouring in the drink absinthe?

    A Mugwort
    B Aniseed
    C Wormwood

11 In the 1980s, Eddie 'The Eagle' Edwards became a household name in which sport?

    A Bungee Jumping
    B Ski Jumping
    C High Jumping

12 Who won a Golden Globe for the song *You'll Be In My Heart* from Disney's *Tarzan*?

    A Elton John
    B Tim Rice
    C Phil Collins

A 108

1	C
2	C
3	C
4	B
5	A
6	B
7	C
8	C
9	A
10	B
11	B
12	C

1 What do *Fanny Hill*, *The Ballad of Reading Gaol* and *Mein Kampf* all have in common?

   A Their authors were ruined after sex scandals
   B They were written in prison
   C Their authors were left-handed

2 What was the first video ever shown on MTV?

   A Blondie's *Heart Of Glass*
   B The Buggles' *Video Killed The Radio Star*
   C Bonnie Tyler's *Total Eclipse Of The Heart*

3 Celtic, Ansated and Maltese are all types of what?

   A Knot
   B Cross
   C Harp

4 How many players are there on a basketball team?

   A Five
   B Six
   C Seven

5 Which artist shot and killed himself while painting *Wheatfield With Crows*?

   A Salvador Dali
   B Vincent Van Gogh
   C Pablo Picasso

6 Which of these composers was NOT born in 1685?

   A Handel
   B Bach
   C Telemann

7 Who plays the foppish Gilderoy Lockhart in *Harry Potter And The Chamber of Secrets?*

   A Kenneth Branagh
   B Hugh Grant
   C Alan Rickman

8 What is shouted in warning of a stray or mis-hit shot on the golf course?

   A Bogey!
   B Fore!
   C Get Out Of The Way!

9 What was the name of the rocky hill that dominated the skyline of ancient Athens?

   A The Acropolis
   B The Parthenon
   C Athene

10 What gang were Butch Cassidy and the Sundance Kid holed up with?

   A The Hole In The Floor Gang
   B The Hole In The Wall Gang
   C The Hole In The Ground Gang

11 Which flower does the expensive spice saffron come from?

   A Poppy
   B Crocus
   C Orchid

12 The hottest temperature in the solar system was recorded on which planet?

   A Mercury
   B Venus
   C Mars

1 **C**
2 **B**
3 **C**
4 **A**
5 **A**
6 **A**
7 **C**
8 **C**
9 **A**
10 **C**
11 **B**
12 **C**

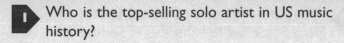

1 Who is the top-selling solo artist in US music history?

   A Elvis Presley
   B Frank Sinatra
   C Garth Brooks

---

2 Who played pop star Curt Wild in *Velvet Goldmine*?

   A Ewan McGregor
   B Christian Bale
   C Jonathan Rhys Meyers

---

3 Which of the following planets has the longest day?

   A Mercury
   B Venus
   C Earth

---

4 In Monopoly, how much does Old Kent Road cost?

   A £20
   B £40
   C £60

---

5 What on an animal is a scut?

   A Tail
   B Claw
   C Nose

---

6 What first did 25-year-old Ellen MacArthur achieve in 2001?

   A Winning the Whitbread prize with her first novel
   B Youngest woman to sail solo around the world
   C Longest-ever horseback ride dressed in full armour

7 What is the full name of the computer image file jpg?

    A Just Processed Gateway bitmap image
    B Joint Photographic Experts Group bitmap image
    C Job Printable Graphics bitmap image

8 When *Fawlty Towers* was shown on Spanish TV, what was Manuel's nationality changed to?

    A Italian
    B French
    C Portuguese

9 Which river runs through the Grand Canyon?

    A The Rio Grande
    B The Colorado
    C No river runs through it

10 Who were the first British team to win a European trophy?

    A Manchester United
    B Celtic
    C Tottenham Hotspur

11 What would you do with a chorizo?

    A Eat it
    B Dance to it
    C Wear it on your head

12 For how long was Lady Jane Grey queen of England?

    A 14 months
    B Nine days
    C Six weeks

A 110

1 B
2 B
3 B
4 A
5 B
6 C
7 A
8 B
9 A
10 B
11 B
12 B

1 What decibel is the threshold level for human hearing?

    A 0
    B 10
    C 100

2 For which charity did S Club 7 record *Never Had A Dream Come True*?

    A Childline
    B Save The Children
    C Children In Need

3 Caracas is the capital city of which country?

    A Peru
    B Venezuela
    C Trinidad and Tobago

4 What was the name of the submarine captain in the novel *20,000 Leagues Under The Sea*?

    A Captain Nemo
    B Captain Ahab
    C Captain Pugwash

5 Which city do football team and sporting club Benfica come from?

    A Lisbon
    B Turin
    C Salamanca

6 Which film begins with the word 'f*ck' repeated several times in succession?

    A *Once Upon A Time In America*
    B *American Psycho*
    C *Four Weddings And A Funeral*

7 What was former prime minister Margaret Thatcher's maiden name?

    A Williams
    B Roberts
    C Jones

8 With which art movement are the French painters Cezanne, Degas, Monet and Renoir associated?

    A Expressionism
    B Impressionism
    C Cubism

9 Why was one of Christopher Columbus's sailors jailed by the Inquisition?

    A For declaring the world was round, not flat
    B For missing Mass every Sunday for 11 months
    C For smoking in public

10 In the traditional children's rhyme, with what was Cock Robin killed?

    A A bow and arrow
    B A snare
    C A stone

11 Which Hindu god is known as the protector of the universe?

    A Brahma
    B Shiva
    C Vishnu

12 What was the first city in the southern hemisphere to host the Olympic Games?

    A Melbourne
    B Sydney
    C Buenos Aires

A
111

1	C
2	A
3	B
4	C
5	A
6	B
7	B
8	A
9	B
10	C
11	A
12	B

1 In which university city would you find Gonville & Caius College and the Fitzwilliam Museum?

    A Oxford
    B Cambridge
    C St Andrews

2 Which of the following is not a real skateboarding trick?

    A The Worm
    B Hand plant
    C Ollie

3 What is the most common British pub name?

    A The Crown
    B The Red Lion
    C The White Horse

4 What is the only way that an object's velocity can be constant?

    A If the object is accelerating
    B If the object is not accelerating
    C If force is applied

5 1st January was adopted as New Year's Day in 1752. What date was New Year's Day until then?

    A 25th March
    B 1st November
    C 25th December

6 *Kids In America* was the first hit for which artist?

    A Mel and Kim
    B Kirsty McColl
    C Kim Wilde

7 *You've Got A Friend In Me* was the theme song of which classic Disney animation?

    A *Toy Story*
    B *The Lion King*
    C *A Bug's Life*

8 When was impressment, or forced recruiting, banned in Britain?

    A 1832
    B 1901
    C It has never been banned

9 What is a wraith?

    A A female spirit whose wailing signals death
    B A mischievous spirit that moves objects around
    C A person's apparition that appears before they die

10 How many players on a netball team are allowed to score?

    A Seven
    B Two
    C One

11 Which British king spent the first eight years of his reign as a fugitive?

    A Robert I (the Bruce)
    B Charles II
    C Macbeth

12 In Charles Dickens' *A Christmas Carol*, how many ghosts and spirits visit Scrooge?

    A Four
    B Three
    C One

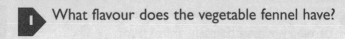

1 What flavour does the vegetable fennel have?

    A Well-rotted fish
    B Aniseed
    C Slightly alcoholic

2 What is the capital of Qatar?

    A Doha
    B Boghi
    C Umm Bab

3 In the binary number system used in computers, what does the number 111 represent?

    A One hundred and eleven
    B Three
    C Seven

4 Which of Henry VIII's wives was Elizabeth I's mother?

    A Catherine of Aragon
    B Anne Boleyn
    C Catherine Howard

5 Who played Schindler in *Schindler's List*?

    A Ralph Fiennes
    B Liam Neeson
    C Ben Kingsley

6 Which of these novels is NOT by Thomas Hardy?

    A *The Mill on the Floss*
    B *The Mayor of Casterbridge*
    C *The Return of the Native*

7 A Talking Heads song title was taken as their name by which band?

   A Smashing Pumpkins
   B Radiohead
   C Human League

8 What are the Honours of Scotland?

   A Scots peers who perform the Queen's state duties
   B The nickname of the Scottish national side
   C The Scottish Crown Jewels

9 In which year did Red Rum win its third Grand National?

   A 1975
   B 1976
   C 1977

10 Which public figure was ruined after a bitter court battle with the Marquis of Queensberry?

   A Writer Oscar Wilde
   B Politician Charles Stewart Parnell
   C Politician Charles Wentworth Dilke

11 Aardvark is an Afrikaans word. What does it mean?

   A Long snout
   B Earth pig
   C Rooter

12 When did Saddam Hussein invade Kuwait, triggering the Gulf War?

   A July 1989
   B August 1990
   C January 1991

1 A Chartreux, a Munchkin and a California Spangled are all types of what?

A Cats
B Cocktails
C Cakes

2 Which Simon and Garfunkel song includes the lines 'People talking without speaking, people listening without hearing'?

A *Mrs Robinson*
B *Sound of Silence*
C *Bridge Over Troubled Water*

3 What was Prince Philip's original surname?

A Mountbatten
B Battenberg
C Panagopoulos

4 Which sport is played at Flushing Meadows?

A Golf
B Archery
C Tennis

5 What arresting ability did the Gorgons of ancient Greek mythology have?

A To turn anyone who looked at them to stone
B To lure sailors onto the rocks by their singing
C To make a man forget his family by their beauty

6 John Prescott was doused with water at the 1998 Brit Awards by a member of which group?

A Oasis
B Chumbawamba
C Pulp

7 Which novel won J K Rowling the 1999 Whitbread Children's Book of the Year award?

   A *Harry Potter and the Philosopher's Stone*
   B *Harry Potter and the Chamber of Secrets*
   C *Harry Potter and the Prisoner of Azkaban*

8 How many islands does Fiji have?

   A 1002
   B 332
   C 14

9 A hit by which Scottish band became the theme song for Quentin Tarantino's *Reservoir Dogs*?

   A Stealers Wheel
   B Nazareth
   C Sutherland Brothers and Quiver

10 Which country hosted its first motor racing Grand Prix in 1999?

   A Japan
   B Malaysia
   C Singapore

11 In which year did the Japanese bomb Pearl Harbor?

   A 1939
   B 1940
   C 1941

12 Which part of the eye is affected by cataracts?

   A Pupil
   B Lens
   C Cornea

1	B
2	A
3	C
4	B
5	B
6	A
7	B
8	C
9	C
10	A
11	B
12	B

1 In Greek mythology, who was the God of the Sea?

A Hades
B Poseidon
C Hermes

2 What is the difference between a frog and a toad?

A A toad is bigger than a frog
B A toad says 'ribbit' and a frog says 'needep'
C A toad walks and a frog hops

3 Who was beaten on the final ball by Dennis Taylor in the 1985 snooker World Championship final?

A Alex Higgins
B Jimmy White
C Steve Davis

4 What is the French name for the English Channel?

A La Manche
B Le Breche Anglaise
C La Tube

5 What is the first day of Lent?

A Good Friday
B Shrove Tuesday
C Ash Wednesday

6 The work of which famous British illustrator featured in Pink Floyd's 1982 film *The Wall*?

A Steve Bell
B Ralph Steadman
C Gerald Scarfe

7 How many rows of stars are there on the American flag?

    A Thirteen
    B Eleven
    C Nine

8 *Saturday Night Fever* soundtrack featured a song by K C And The Sunshine Band. What was it?

    A *That's The Way I Like It*
    B *Get Down Tonight*
    C *Boogie Shoes*

9 How many times did Bjorn Borg win the Men's Singles title at Wimbledon?

    A Three
    B Four
    C Five

10 Who composed the opera *Hansel and Gretel*?

    A Neil Sedaka
    B Engelbert Humperdinck
    C David Cassidy

11 What instrument of modern warfare was first used at the Somme in 1916?

    A The machine gun
    B The tank
    C The bomber plane

12 According to *Aesop's Fables*, who removed a thorn from the paw of a lion?

    A David
    B Daniel
    C Androcles

1	A
2	B
3	B
4	C
5	A
6	B
7	C
8	B
9	A
10	B
11	C
12	B

1 How did King Charles II die?

  A He suffocated in an oak tree
  B He died in his bed
  C He was beheaded

2 What is polyvinyl chloride better known as?

  A Polystyrene
  B PVC
  C Polyfilla

3 How many points is the bullseye worth in outdoor archery?

  A 10
  B 15
  C 25

4 Who co-wrote Elton John's early hits with him?

  A Bernie Taupin
  B John Reid
  C Kiki Dee

5 In which state is the volcano Mount St Helens, which erupted in 1980?

  A Oregon
  B North Dakota
  C Washington

6 There are five Balearic Islands: Mallorca, Menorca, Ibiza and Cabrera. What is the fifth?

  A Formosa
  B Formentera
  C Fuerteventura

7 Who wanted 'To make Britain a fit country for heroes to live in'?

    A Winston Churchill
    B Clement Atlee
    C Lloyd George

8 If a horse were 20 hands high, how tall would it be?

    A 60 inches
    B 80 inches
    C 100 inches

9 What is antimony?

    A A protest against the rich
    B Payment to a separated spouse
    C A brittle silvery-white metal

10 What was notable about the 1972 UEFA Cup final?

    A It was played between two English sides
    B Fans invaded the pitch and stopped play
    C The presentation was held up as the cup was lost

11 What type of character is Mrs Tiggywinkle?

    A An aged but good-hearted crone
    B A hedgehog
    C The proprietor of a dolls' hospital

12 What was unusual about the angel Metatron in the movie *Dogma*?

    A He had no voice
    B He had no body
    C He had no genitals

A
116

1 **B**
2 **C**
3 **C**
4 **A**
5 **C**
6 **C**
7 **C**
8 **C**
9 **C**
10 **B**
11 **B**
12 **C**

239

1 The Mesozoic era is divided into three geological periods. Cretaceous and Jurassic are two. What is the third?

A Carboniferous
B Triassic
C Silurian

2 What was the original name of The Pogues?

A The Nips
B Pogue Mahone
C The Popes

3 In which sport can competitors be disqualified for 'timber-topping'?

A Hurdles
B Tossing the Caber
C World Speed Tree-Felling Championships

4 Which famous actor appeared in the chorus line of *South Pacific*'s original London run?

A Sean Connery
B Michael Caine
C Malcolm McDowell

5 What is the sum of the degrees in the internal angles of a triangle?

A 360
B 180
C 90

6 What is the English equivalent of the German Rathaus?

A Beer cellar
B Town hall
C Sewer

7 What symbol represents a battlefield on an Ordnance Survey map?

A A cannon
B Crossed swords
C A flag

8 Who followed Val Kilmer into the Batmobile?

A George Clooney
B Michael Keaton
C Toby Maguire

9 Who was named FIFA World Player of the Year in December 2003?

A Ronaldo
B Thierry Henry
C Zinedine Zidane

10 What do linen, bronze, silk and silver all have in common?

A All share the same basic chemical formula
B All had to be used in medieval church decoration
C All are wedding anniversaries

11 In 1785, Blanchard and Jeffries became the first to cross the English Channel by which means?

A Steamboat
B Balloon
C Inflatable dinghy

12 What are dried plums known as?

A Raisins
B Dried plums
C Prunes

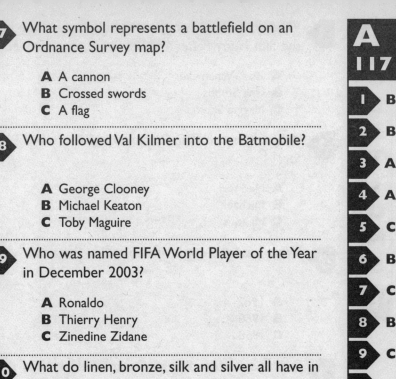

1 B
2 B
3 A
4 A
5 C
6 B
7 C
8 B
9 C
10 A
11 B
12 C

241

1 Who starred as flying teacher Madam Hooch in the film *Harry Potter And The Philosopher's Stone?*

A Zoe Wanamaker
B Una Stubbs
C Maggie Smith

2 What does the M in Richard M Nixon stand for?

A Madison
B Michael
C Milhous

3 What year did conscription end in Britain?

A 1962
B 1960
C 1958

4 Patriotism, according to Oscar Wilde, is the virtue of whom?

A The virtuous
B The vicious
C The victorious

5 Who was Don McLean's song *American Pie* about?

A The Beatles
B Buddy Holly
C Elvis Presley

6 What is the capital of Moldova?

A Tbilisi
B Chisinau
C Ljubljana

7 Who first argued that the world was not flat?

   A The explorer Magellan
   B The scientist Galileo
   C The philosopher Aristotle

8 Which German footballer's nickname was 'Der Bomber'?

   A Franz Beckenbauer
   B Karl-Heinz Rummenigge
   C Gerd Muller

9 The body of the Egyptian Sphinx is based on which animal?

   A Lion
   B Cat
   C Camel

10 If a car has the nationality badge 'IS', where does it come from?

   A Iceland
   B Indonesia
   C Israel

11 Which well-known artist had a pet monkey?

   A Jackson Pollock
   B Emily Carr
   C Andy Warhol

12 What does the word 'biopic' mean?

   A Able to see clearly with both eyes
   B A film about someone's life
   C An examination of skin with a microscope

243

1 In astronomy, what is a 'brown dwarf'?

A A star which has burnt itself out
B A star which is outshone by a brighter neighbour
C A star which never gains enough mass to shine

2 With whom did Phil Oakey record *Together In Electric Dreams* in 1984?

A The Human League
B Giorgio Moroder
C Gary Numan

3 Which country has the most land preserved for wildlife?

A Greenland
B Australia
C Germany

4 Who played *Buffy the Vampire Slayer* in the original movie?

A Sarah Michelle Gellar
B Kirsty Swanson
C Kirsten Dunst

5 Which town in Britain did the Romans name Aquae Sulis?

A Cheltenham
B Leamington Spa
C Bath

6 By what name is Arthur Jefferson better known?

A Buster Keaton
B Rudolph Valentino
C Stan Laurel

7 Why did Adolf Hitler hurriedly leave Berlin's Olympic Stadium during the 1936 games?

    A To avoid an SS commander with a similar uniform
    B To avoid presenting medals to a black athlete
    C To avoid the British ambassador

8 Which modern author has written a popular series of vampire novels?

    A Christopher Brookmyre
    B Anne Rice
    C Zadie Smith

9 What does the name 'Mississippi' mean?

    A Big river
    B Muddy river
    C River of blood

10 Colin McRae is the only Brit to be world champion in which sport?

    A Motor Racing
    B World Rally
    C Formula 3000 racing

11 Which African state was founded by freed American slaves?

    A Sierra Leone
    B The Gambia
    C Liberia

12 Which country's teams have won the European Cup more often than any others?

    A Spain's
    B Germany's
    C Italy's

A
119

1 A
2 C
3 A
4 B
5 B
6 B
7 C
8 C
9 A
10 A
11 B
12 B

1 In the original *Star Trek* series, what was First Engineer Mr Scott's first name?

   A Jocky
   B Montgomery
   C James

2 Which English football club won the European Cup in 1984?

   A Liverpool
   B Manchester United
   C Aston Villa

3 Who first sailed solo around the world from east to west, against the winds and currents?

   A Francis Chichester
   B Chay Blyth
   C Alain Colas

4 What is the boiling point of water in degrees Fahrenheit?

   A 212
   B 186
   C 100

5 Who, according to one commentator, 'disguised his popery to the last'?

   A John Wayne
   B Charles II
   C Pope Pius XII

6 What do the drummers from Queen and Duran Duran have in common?

   A They both have four fingers on their left hand
   B They both have the same name
   C Neither could play when their groups were formed

7 Which country ruled the Ottoman Empire until the First World War?

    A Hungary
    B Russia
    C Turkey

8 What does an entymologist study?

    A Insects
    B Words
    C Fish

9 Only one living British boxer has been inducted into the USA Boxing Hall of Fame. Who is he?

    A Henry Cooper
    B Ken Buchanan
    C Lennox Lewis

10 Most of the days of the week are named after Pagan gods; from which mythology?

    A Celtic
    B Roman
    C Norse

11 Where was the movie *Trainspotting* mostly filmed?

    A Glasgow
    B London
    C Edinburgh

12 Which American author created the characters Rip Van Winkle and Ichabod Crane?

    A Nathaniel Hawthorne
    B Washington Irving
    C Mark Twain

A 120

1	C
2	B
3	A
4	B
5	C
6	C
7	B
8	B
9	A
10	B
11	C
12	A

247

1 Which band sang with Skinner and Baddiel on *Three Lions* in 1998?

    A Ocean Colour Scene
    B The Lightning Seeds
    C The Beautiful South

2 What is the pejorative term for an Irish person with English affectations?

    A A West Brit
    B An eejit
    C A Hibernophobe

3 Who said, 'The English have no exalted sentiments: they can all be bought'?

    A Napoleon Bonaparte
    B FIFA Vice-President Chung Mong-Joon of S Korea
    C American President George W. Bush

4 The film *Ten Things I Hate About You* was loosely based on which literary classic?

    A Jane Austin's *Emma*
    B Shakespeare's *The Taming Of The Shrew*
    C George Eliot's *Middlemarch*

5 For what are the Lascaux Caves in France famous?

    A Dinosaur fossils
    B Enormous stalactites
    C Prehistoric wall paintings

6 Ermine coats are made from the fur of which creature?

    A Mink
    B Rat
    C Stoat

7 What is the second-last letter of the Greek alphabet?

    A Psi
    B Sigma
    C Omega

8 Who is the only Scotsman ever to have captained the England cricket team?

    A Mike Brearley
    B Mike Atherton
    C Mike Denness

9 If you sprinkled NaCl on your food, what effect would it have?

    A Flavour it
    B Poison it
    C Turn it yellow

10 When was the American Civil War?

    A 1775–1783
    B 1812–1815
    C 1861–1865

11 The actor Jon Voigt is the father of which Oscar-winning actress?

    A Angelina Jolie
    B Melanie Griffith
    C Jodie Foster

12 The traditional French 'fines herbes' blend has chervil, chives, tarragon, and another. What is it?

    A Dill
    B Parsley
    C Rosemary

A
121

1 **B**
2 **A**
3 **B**
4 **A**
5 **B**
6 **B**
7 **C**
8 **A**
9 **B**
10 **C**
11 **A**
12 **B**

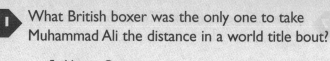

Q (vertical) **U E S T I O N S 123**

1 What British boxer was the only one to take Muhammad Ali the distance in a world title bout?

   A Henry Cooper
   B Richard Dunn
   C Joe Bugner

2 Which cricketer had the highest-ever run-making average in his test career?

   A Gary Sobers
   B Don Bradman
   C Herbert Sutcliffe

3 How many panels are there on a football?

   A 28
   B 32
   C 36

4 Who played the vampire in the classic 1922 film *Nosferatu*?

   A Max Schreck
   B Lon Chaney
   C Bela Lugosi

5 Who invented the sport of lacrosse?

   A The Native Americans
   B The Vikings
   C The Polynesians

6 Who was the first person to tell the Americans, 'The British are coming!'?

   A Colin Welland
   B Paul Revere
   C George Washington

7 In the classic children's TV show *Daktari*, what was so unusual about Clarence the lion?

    A He only had three legs
    B He was cross-eyed
    C He was stuffed

8 If you dropped a feather and a cannonball in a vacuum at the same time, which would land first?

    A The cannonball
    B Both would land at the same time
    C Both would float

9 Which is the biggest state in the USA?

    A Texas
    B Alaska
    C California

10 What was The Jam's final single?

    A *Town Called Malice*
    B *Solid Bond In Your Heart*
    C *Beat Surrender*

11 How did the tuxedo get its name?

    A From its designer, Roberto Tuxedo
    B From the place it was first worn in New York
    C From the Portuguese word for 'penguin'

12 After Shakespeare, who is the second most published author ever in the English language?

    A Barbara Cartland
    B Catherine Cookson
    C Charles Dickens

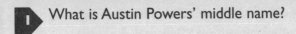

1 What is Austin Powers' middle name?

A Randy
B Bond
C Danger

2 The Berlioz opera *Béatrice et Bénédict* was based on a Shakespeare play. Which one?

A *The Taming of the Shrew*
B *Much Ado About Nothing*
C *The Merry Wives of Windsor*

3 In the USA, the 1925 Scopes Trial was a landmark case. What was it about?

A The freedom of the press
B The teaching of evolution in schools
C Allowing prayer in non-private schools

4 What is Paul Hewson better known as?

A The Edge
B Bono
C Dave Evans

5 Which caring professionals have the caduceus as their emblem?

A Dentists
B Chiropodists
C Doctors

6 Which popular stand-up comic is a qualified doctor?

A Harry Hill
B Eddie Izzard
C Dylan Moran

7 If an Australian came across a bitzer, what would he or she be looking at?

    A An outback town
    B A mongrel
    C A Vegemite sandwich

8 What was significant about Fahrenheit 451 in the Ray Bradbury novel of the same name?

    A It's the temperature that melts human flesh
    B It's the temperature that combusts book paper
    C It's the temperature that explodes the Earth

9 Seve Ballesteros won The Open three times, twice at the same course. Which one?

    A Royal Lytham
    B St Andrews
    C Muirfield

10 Two Greek gods were twins. One was Artemis, goddess of the moon. Who was the other?

    A Apollo
    B Aphrodite
    C Athene

11 How many people have walked on the Moon?

    A 10
    B 12
    C 14

12 Which Renaissance artist is more known for his published work than for his art?

    A Fra Angelico
    B Da Vinci
    C Vasari

A
1 2 3

1	C
2	B
3	B
4	A
5	A
6	B
7	B
8	B
9	B
10	C
11	B
12	C

1 From which language does the word 'tattoo' come?

    A Hindustani
    B Tahitian
    C Arabic

2 What was the name of the US attempt to crack Japanese codes during the Second World War?

    A MAGIC
    B BANZAI
    C ULTRA

3 Who is drag performer Paul O'Grady better known as?

    A Danny La Rue
    B Lily Savage
    C Ru Paul

4 Which of the following was not one of the surrogate fathers in the film *Three Men And A Baby*?

    A Billy Crystal
    B Ted Danson
    C Tom Selleck

5 What years were English football clubs banned from European competition?

    A 1986–1991
    B 1984–1991
    C 1985–1991

6 Of the two sex chromosomes X and Y, which two combine to form a male?

    A XX
    B YY
    C XY

7 Who wrote the children's stories *The Ugly Duckling* and *The Emperor's New Clothes*?

    A Hans Christian Andersen
    B The Brothers Grimm
    C Oscar Wilde

8 Which is Britain's largest area of fresh water?

    A Lake Windermere
    B Loch Lomond
    C Loch Ness

9 On the ninth day of Christmas, what did my true love send to me?

    A Nine lords a-leaping
    B Nine maids a-milking
    C Nine drummers drumming

10 What item of clothing was outlawed in Turkey in 1925?

    A The hijab (head covering)
    B The kaftan
    C The fez

11 What is a centaur?

    A Half-human, half-bull
    B Half-horse, half-griffin
    C Half-horse, half-human

12 Which FBI agent replaced Fox Mulder as Dana Scully's partner in later series of *The X-Files*?

    A John Doggett
    B Walter Skinner
    C Robert Patrick

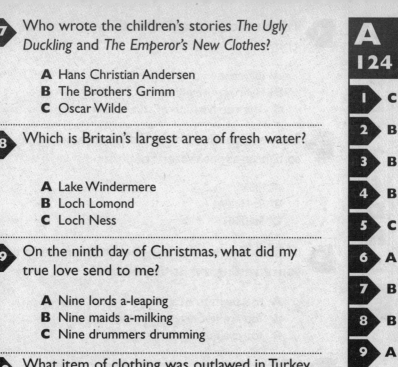

A 124

1	C
2	B
3	B
4	B
5	C
6	A
7	B
8	B
9	A
10	A
11	B
12	C

1 What makes farts smell?

   A Methane
   B Hydrogen sulphide
   C The combination of several digestive gases

2 From which island exile did Napoleon escape to fight again at Waterloo?

   A Elba
   B St Helena
   C Sardinia

3 In Cockney rhyming slang, what is happening if you're getting the Britney Spears?

   A You seem to be having difficulty hearing
   B You are not driving the car smoothly
   C You are buying the next round

4 Which drug comes from the bark of the cinchona tree?

   A Cocaine
   B Aspirin
   C Quinine

5 John F. Kennedy was the last US President to be assassinated. Who was the first?

   A Abraham Lincoln
   B William McKinley
   C James Garfield

6 What was 'heading west' in The Stranglers' 1982 single *Golden Brown*?

   A Heroin
   B Cinnamon
   C Syphilis

7 What does the term 'brut' mean when referring to wine?

    A Unpleasant
    B Very dry
    C Smells of flowers

8 In ancient Rome, what colour of robes did public servants wear?

    A Blue
    B Brown
    C Red

9 What nationality was Nobel Prize-winning scientist Marie Curie?

    A French
    B Polish
    C Russian

10 What colour of jersey is given to the best climber in the Mountains stage of the Tour de France?

    A Yellow
    B Green
    C White with big red polka dots

11 Which blonde actress was never married to film director Roger Vadim?

    A Anita Ekberg
    B Brigitte Bardot
    C Jane Fonda

12 If you sent a friend a secret message online, how might you head it?

    A MYOB
    B RFI
    C FYEO

1 Who wrote the early science fiction novel *The Lost World*?

A H.G. Wells
B Jules Verne
C Arthur Conan Doyle

2 Which film featured the biggest number of extras ever used in one scene?

A *War And Peace*
B *Ben Hur*
C *Gandhi*

3 How is the ball hit in the game of pelota?

A With long-handled hammers
B With the hand
C With squash-racket-like sticks

4 Which Soviet city withstood a Nazi siege that killed over 640,000 people from 1941 to 1942?

A St Petersburg
B Stalingrad
C Leningrad

5 Which celebrity TV cook is the Chairperson of Norwich City FC?

A Jamie Oliver
B Delia Smith
C Gary Rhodes

6 Which city was the English capital before London?

A York
B Winchester
C Oxford

7 What is the standard temperature of the human body?

  A 36.4°C
  B 37°C
  C 37.6°C

8 What instruction on a piece of classical music shows the point where a voice comes in?

  A Voce
  B Solo
  C Concerto

9 What does the suffix 'stan' mean when it appears in the name of a nation, such as Turkmenistan?

  A Republic of
  B Land of
  C Newly free

10 In Greek mythology, what was the name of the goddess Hera's hundred-eyed watchman?

  A Centioculus
  B Cyclops
  C Argus

11 How many cigars did British PM Winston Churchill ration himself to per day?

  A 6
  B 12
  C 15

12 Which *Blackadder* cast member wrote the children's TV series *Maid Marian And Her Merry Men*?

  A Tim McInnery
  B Rowan Atkinson
  C Tony Robinson

1 When was Pompeii destroyed by the eruption of Mount Vesuvius?

    A 33 AD
    B 79 AD
    C 101 AD

2 What is the first book in the New Testament?

    A Gospel of Matthew
    B Acts of the Apostles
    C Revelation

3 Before Goran Ivanisevic in 2002, who was the last Wimbledon champion not to defend his title?

    A Jimmy Connors
    B John Newcombe
    C Stan Smith

4 What is the ingredient in cola that rots human teeth?

    A Sugar
    B Caramel
    C Phosphoric acid

5 Which of his cartoon characters did Walt Disney provide the original voice of?

    A Donald Duck
    B Mickey Mouse
    C Goofy

6 How many times was Eric Bristow, the Crafty Cockney, World Darts champion?

    A Five
    B Seven
    C Eleven

7 Which chemical element has the symbol W?

   A Tungsten
   B Mercury
   C Potassium

8 Who were the original Levellers?

   A A political movement in the American Civil War
   B A political group in the British Civil Wars
   C A folk-punk band from the 80s and 90s

9 What is a hippophobe afraid of?

   A Fish
   B Horses
   C Hippopotamuses

10 Who is on the verge of smashing his guitar on the cover of The Clash's album *London Calling*?

   A Joe Strummer
   B Paul Simonon
   C Mick Jones

11 How many symphonies did Joseph Haydn compose?

   A 104
   B 84
   C 64

12 Angstrom, tilde and breve are all types of what?

   A Musical notes
   B Saltwater fish
   C Accents

A
127

1 C
2 C
3 B
4 C
5 B
6 B
7 B
8 A
9 B
10 C
11 C
12 C

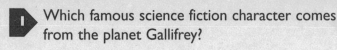

1 Which famous science fiction character comes from the planet Gallifrey?

A Doctor Who
B Zaphod Beeblebrox
C Luke Skywalker

2 Two members of the Beatles were left handed; which two?

A Paul McCartney and John Lennon
B Paul McCartney and Ringo Starr
C Paul McCartney and George Harrison

3 What did the dog do to the cat in *The House That Jack Built*?

A Ate it
B Chased it
C Worried it

4 What are the three green properties on the Monopoly board?

A Mayfair, Park Lane and Regent Street
B Regent Street, Bond Street and Oxford Street
C Bond Street, Oxford Street and Piccadilly

5 If you were to spread out a pair of lungs, how big would their surface area be?

A The size of a double duvet
B The size of an average living-room
C The size of a tennis court

6 Who recorded an album called *Blonde On Blonde*?

A Texas
B Bob Dylan
C Bucks Fizz

7 Who was the last British king to die in battle?

    A James IV of Scotland
    B Richard III of England
    C James III of Scotland

8 Which series of films has had more sequels than any other?

    A *Godzilla*
    B *The Carry Ons*
    C *Charlie Chan*

9 In which sport do Glasgow Hawks, Heriots FP and Gala play?

    A Curling
    B Shinty
    C Rugby

10 In Greek mythology, what was left in Pandora's Box after she released Misery and Evil?

    A Hope
    B Love
    C Faith

11 What happens to toilet waste on board aeroplanes?

    A It is jettisoned with each flush
    B It is recycled to provide extra fuel
    C It is stored on board until the flight ends

12 What artist and filmmaker set Marilyn Monroe's likeness on a series of silkscreen prints?

    A Roy Lichtenstein
    B Andy Warhol
    C Luis Buñuel

A
128

1	B
2	A
3	C
4	C
5	B
6	A
7	A
8	B
9	B
10	B
11	A
12	C

263

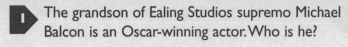

1 The grandson of Ealing Studios supremo Michael Balcon is an Oscar-winning actor. Who is he?

   A Daniel Day-Lewis
   B Ralph Fiennes
   C Kenneth Branagh

2 After which famous historical figure was the teddy bear named?

   A Composer Edward Elgar
   B US President Theodore Roosevelt
   C King Edward VII

3 How many stars are there in Orion's belt in the night sky?

   A Five
   B Eight
   C Three

4 Which important Christian site is governed by the Palestinian Authority?

   A Bethlehem
   B Nazareth
   C Jerusalem

5 Apart from cricket, which sport did Viv Richards play for Antigua at international level?

   A Football
   B Squash
   C Athletics

6 Who or what do the Swiss Guard protect?

   A The Swiss President
   B The Pope
   C The Italian–Swiss borders

7 Which Aegean island was devastated over 3,500 years ago by an enormous volcanic eruption?

    A Crete
    B Santorini
    C Mykonos

8 Who picked up an Oscar for *Monsters Ball* in 2002?

    A Halle Berry
    B Denzel Washington
    C Billy Bob Thornton

9 Who did France beat to win Euro 2000?

    A Italy
    B Sweden
    C Germany

10 What is the American slang word for five cents?

    A Nickel
    B Dime
    C Quarter

11 In 1963, 3 singles entered the UK charts at no. 1. Two were by the Beatles; whose was the third?

    A The Rolling Stones
    B Elvis Presley
    C The Who

12 Which fruit used to be called a 'love apple'?

    A Peach
    B Tomato
    C Fig

1	A
2	B
3	C
4	B
5	C
6	A
7	A
8	B
9	C
10	A
11	C
12	B

1 Transylvania is part of which country?

   A Russia
   B Bulgaria
   C Romania

2 At which racecourse is the French Classic the Prix de l'Arc de Triomphe run?

   A Longchamp
   B Chantilly
   C Saint-Cloud

3 Which Crimean War battle gave its name to an article of clothing?

   A Anorak
   B Cardigan
   C Balaclava

4 Who were the first people to see the resurrected Christ?

   A A group of Roman soldiers
   B Peter and John the Apostles
   C Mary Magdalene and her two friends

5 To date, how many Irishmen have won the Nobel Prize for Literature?

   A Two
   B Three
   C Four

6 Which cult TV show featured characters Sharon Macready, Richard Barrett and Craig Stirling?

   A *The Persuaders*
   B *The Champions*
   C *The Tomorrow People*

7 How many sides does a 20p piece have?

A Five
B Six
C Seven

8 Who wrote *The Third Man*?

A George Orwell
B Graham Greene
C Evelyn Waugh

9 How did Queen Cleopatra of Egypt die?

A She suffocated in a rolled-up carpet
B She was bitten by an asp
C She drowned in a bath of asses' milk

10 What energy value is one horsepower?

A 745.7 watts
B 7457 watts
C 74,574 watts

11 Who won an Oscar for his role in the 1973 film *Save the Tiger*?

A Gene Hackman
B Jack Lemmon
C Jack Nicholson

12 When were Australian Aboriginal native peoples granted citizenship of Australia?

A 1788
B 1918
C 1967

1 What was the name of Henry VIII's warship that sank in the Solent in 1545?

   A The Great Michael
   B The Mary Rose
   C The Fair Maid

2 Whom did Andrew Motion succeed as Poet Laureate in 1999?

   A John Betjeman
   B Ted Hughes
   C Philip Larkin

3 Which one of the Three Musketeers ultimately entered the priesthood?

   A Athos
   B Porthos
   C Aramis

4 What is the maximum number of clubs allowed in a golf bag?

   A 12
   B 14
   C 17

5 Who is the richest living British musician?

   A Elton John
   B Paul McCartney
   C Andrew Lloyd Webber

6 Gone With the Wind, Stagecoach and The Wizard Of Oz competed for Best Picture Oscar in what year?

   A 1938
   B 1939
   C 1940

7 What is the Dewey Decimal System?

    A A method of calculating rainfall in the UK
    B A library system for classifying books
    C The UK's decimal coinage system

8 What is an alligator pear better known as?

    A Avocado
    B Mango
    C Papaya

9 In which sport do competitors perform a Randi, a Seat Drop and a Flatback?

    A Synchronised swimming
    B Bobsleighing
    C Trampolining

10 Which successful musician married Cait O'Riordan of the Pogues?

    A Shane McGowan
    B Billy Bragg
    C Elvis Costello

11 When was the last execution by guillotine in France?

    A 1921
    B 1946
    C 1977

12 What is a Chinese Uncle?

    A A Japanese wartime torture device
    B A vodka and dry-ginger cocktail
    C A type of sailing ship

1	C
2	A
3	C
4	C
5	C
6	B
7	C
8	B
9	B
10	A
11	B
12	C

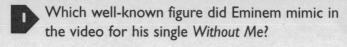

QUESTIONS

133

1 Which well-known figure did Eminem mimic in the video for his single *Without Me*?

  A Adolf Hitler
  B Joe Stalin
  C Osama Bin Laden

2 Which creature has teeth in its stomach?

  A Lobster
  B Tarantula
  C Boa constrictor

3 Which Irish writer told of the 'terrible beauty' born at Easter 1916?

  A Sean O'Casey
  B W.B. Yeats
  C James Joyce

4 How many British Prime Ministers have been assassinated?

  A None
  B One
  C Two

5 If you had read 30% of a 370-page book, how many pages would you have read?

  A 123 pages
  B 127 pages
  C 111 pages

6 By what name is Edson Arantes do Nascimento better known?

  A Pele
  B Eusebio
  C Ronaldo

7 What did Queen Elizabeth do for the first time in April 1993?

    A Opened up Buckingham Palace to the public
    B Paid income tax
    C Received the PM for tea every Wednesday

8 What was the name of Data's cat in *Star Trek: The Next Generation*?

    A Kirk
    B Spot
    C Spock

9 What condition would you have if you have hypermetropia?

    A Longsightedness
    B High blood pressure
    C Erratic heartbeat

10 Why did Pickles the dog shoot to fame in 1966?

    A He ran on to the pitch during a World Cup tie
    B He peed on Alf Ramsay's shoes during the final
    C He found the World Cup after it was stolen

11 Who was Ireland's greatest mythological hero?

    A Darby O'Gill
    B Finnegan
    C Cuchulain

12 In the song *The Wheels On The Bus*, what does the driver do?

    A Drives all around town
    B Says, 'Move along, please'
    C Takes all the money

A

132

1	B
2	B
3	C
4	B
5	B
6	B
7	B
8	A
9	C
10	C
11	C
12	B

1 What is the proper name of the painting generally known as *Whistler's Mother*?

    A *Arrangement In Black And Grey*
    B *Mother In A Chair*
    C *Putting Your Feet Up*

2 Which city has the oldest underground railway in the world?

    A Paris
    B New York
    C London

3 What is a dendrologist?

    A Someone who collects roadsigns
    B Someone who specialises in scalp diseases
    C Someone who studies trees and shrubs

4 By what name was Frances Gumm more glamorously known?

    A Jane Russell
    B Judy Garland
    C Jayne Mansfield

5 Coca-Cola originally contained extracts of which drug?

    A Aspirin
    B Opium
    C Cocaine

6 Which cocktail consists of Tia Maria, vodka and coke?

    A Screwdriver
    B Black Russian
    C Mexican Hat Dance

7 When was the Domesday Book compiled?

    A 1066
    B 1086
    C 1072

8 What is the only gemstone that is composed of a single element?

    A Diamond
    B Moonstone
    C Sapphire

9 Singers Annie Lennox and Shane McGowan share a birthday; what day is it?

    A April Fool's Day
    B New Year's Day
    C Christmas Day

10 Who is the only player to have scored in every round of a World Cup, including the final?

    A Gerd Muller
    B Jairzinho
    C Eusebio

11 Which Italian city is home to the Uffizi art gallery?

    A Florence
    B Bologna
    C Turin

12 When Disney's seven dwarfs set off to work, what are they mining for?

    A Gold
    B Diamonds
    C Coal

1 What Australian rock band featured on the soundtrack to the Nicholas Cage film *Face/Off*?

   A The Saints
   B AC/DC
   C INXS

2 Which country scored the first-ever golden goal at the World Cup finals?

   A France
   B South Korea
   C Senegal

3 What was the name of the old man who narrated the Brer Rabbit stories?

   A Uncle Fester
   B Uncle Remus
   C Uncle Romulus

4 How many characters did Alastair Sim play in *Kind Hearts and Coronets*?

   A None
   B One
   C Eight

5 What is hypnophobia the fear of?

   A Sleep
   B Being hypnotised
   C Being laughed at

6 Which American sporting legend was known as Joltin' Joe?

   A Joe Montana
   B Joe Di Maggio
   C Joe Namath

7 In the classic TV show *The Simpsons*, what is the name of the barkeeper?

  A Barney
  B Ned
  C Moe

8 Whose finger is Adam's pointed to on the ceiling of the Sistine Chapel?

  A Lucifer
  B God
  C Eve

9 In ancient Egypt, scarab amulets were associated with resurrection. What was a scarab shaped like?

  A Cat
  B Jackal
  C Dung beetle

10 Why did the late-80s duo Milli Vanilli have to hand back their Best New Artist Grammy?

  A For not having sung on any of their records
  B For calling the awards committee 'boring old farts'
  C For having been in four other bands before

11 Which country was ruled by King Zog in the 1930s?

  A Albania
  B Romania
  C Hungary

12 If a pound of butter were taken to Jupiter, how much would it weigh there?

  A 0.254 pound
  B 2.54 pounds
  C 25.4 pounds

A
134

1 A
2 C
3 C
4 B
5 C
6 B
7 B
8 A
9 C
10 B
11 A
12 B

1 Sirius, the brightest star of all, is in which constellation?

   A Canis Major
   B Corona Borealis
   C Scorpius

2 What was the name of Arthur Dent's alien friend in *The Hitchhiker's Guide To The Galaxy*?

   A Ford Anglia
   B Ford Prefect
   C Ford Cortina

3 In Chicago's 1929 St Valentine's Day Massacre, what were Al Capone's hitmen dressed as?

   A Cupids
   B Policemen
   C Stripograms

4 Who is the only Canadian to have won the World Snooker championship to date?

   A Kirk Stevens
   B Bill Werbeniuk
   C Cliff Thorburn

5 The first nativity scene was displayed in 1223; by whom?

   A Pope Innocent III
   B St Francis of Assisi
   C Archbishop Thomas Becket

6 Six characters in the Village People are: biker, cop, cowboy, Indian and sailor. What is the seventh?

   A Construction worker
   B Swimmer
   C Soldier

7 What nationality was the explorer Christopher Columbus?

    A Portuguese
    B Spanish
    C Italian

8 Which of the following clouds would you expect to rain on you?

    A Cirrus
    B Cirrocumulus
    C Cumulonimbus

9 Who played the voice of Shrek in the movie of the same name?

    A Mike Myers
    B Eddie Murphy
    C John Lithgow

10 Who was the victim in what is usually seen as the first live televised murder?

    A Bobby Kennedy
    B John F. Kennedy
    C Lee Harvey Oswald

11 How long did it take to build Notre Dame cathedral in Paris?

    A 182 years
    B 131 years
    C 104 years

12 If a dog barks and a duck quacks, what sound does a deer make?

    A Bray
    B Bell
    C None

A 135

1	C
2	A
3	B
4	A
5	A
6	B
7	C
8	B
9	C
10	A
11	A
12	B

1 In the classic children's TV show *Mary, Mungo and Midge*, what is Mungo?

- **A** A mouse
- **B** A dog
- **C** A cat

2 What American soul-music star was murdered by his father the day before his 45th birthday?

- **A** Junior Walker
- **B** Marvin Gaye
- **C** Curtis Mayfield

3 How many noble, or inert, gases are there?

- **A** Four
- **B** Five
- **C** Six

4 Who is the presenter of the long-running Channel 4 game show *Countdown*?

- **A** Richard Madeley
- **B** Richard Whiteley
- **C** Richard Dimbleby

5 Of whom did Bobby Charlton say, 'He was the greatest player of all time'?

- **A** Alfredo Di Stéfano
- **B** Pele
- **C** Eusebio

6 Who was the Greek god of wine, fertility and ecstasy?

- **A** Dionysus
- **B** Liber
- **C** Bacchus

7 What were the names of the children Mary Poppins looked after?

    A Jane and Peter Brown
    B Jane and Thomas Booth
    C Jane and Michael Banks

8 What was the cause of the 1966 Aberfan disaster, in which 81 schoolchildren died?

    A A fire
    B A plane crash
    C A slag heap collapsed

9 Which country produces more gem diamonds than any other?

    A South Africa
    B Botswana
    C Angola

10 The *Godfather Part III* was partly based on the mysterious death of which real-life pope?

    A Paul VI
    B John Paul
    C John Paul II

11 What is hydrophobia more commonly known as?

    A B. O.
    B Rabies
    C Psoriasis

12 What great French naive painter was also known as Le Douanier Rousseau?

    A Henri Rousseau
    B Jean-Jacques Rousseau
    C Theodore Rousseau

A
136

1	A
2	B
3	B
4	C
5	B
6	A
7	C
8	C
9	A
10	C
11	A
12	B

1 Where is the only place vampire bats can be found?

   A Transylvanian hills and forests
   B Central Asian mountains and forests
   C Central & South American scrub and forests

2 How did Captain Cook die?

   A He was murdered by hostile natives in Hawaii
   B He fell overboard and drowned
   C He was killed by his crew in a mutiny

3 Which make of British bike did Marlon Brando ride in *The Wild One*?

   A Triumph
   B Vincent
   C Norton

4 Which Shakespearean character had a mother called Gertrude?

   A Cordelia
   B Brutus
   C Hamlet

5 From which country does feta cheese come?

   A Bulgaria
   B Greece
   C Portugal

6 What does a BCG vaccine inoculate against?

   A Smallpox
   B TB
   C Mumps, measles and rubella

7 Which bird can fly straight up, down and backwards?

    A Swift
    B Hummingbird
    C Eagle

8 In 3 seconds: How many times does 'p' occur in the first line of the *Peter Piper* tongue twister?

    A Nine
    B Seven
    C Six

9 How many images of individual Beatles feature on the cover of the *Sergeant Pepper* album?

    A Three
    B Four
    C Eight

10 What is the first event in the heptathlon?

    A 100 metres hurdles
    B Javelin
    C 800 metres

11 Death plays chess in the classic *The Seventh Seal*. What 90s parody showed Death playing Twister?

    A *Austin Powers International Man Of Mystery*
    B *Bill & Ted's Bogus Journey*
    C *Time Bandits*

12 Which Sioux leader defeated General Custer to win the Battle of the Little Bighorn in 1876?

    A Sitting Bull
    B Geronimo
    C Crazy Horse

A
137

1 **B**
2 **B**
3 **C**
4 **B**
5 **A**
6 **A**
7 **C**
8 **C**
9 **B**
10 **B**
11 **B**
12 **A**

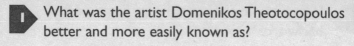

Q **UESTIONS**

139

1 What was the artist Domenikos Theotocopoulos better and more easily known as?

    A Miro
    B El Greco
    C Titian

2 In Harry Potter, the Hogwarts' houses are Ravenclaw, Gryffindor and Slytherin. What is the fourth?

    A Huffenpuff
    B Hufflepuff
    C Hufferpuffer

3 What is the state capital of California?

    A San Francisco
    B San Diego
    C Sacramento

4 If something was 100 fathoms deep, how many feet under the water would it be?

    A 300
    B 600
    C 1,000

5 Who was the first female composer to win an Oscar?

    A Barbra Streisand
    B Carole King
    C Carly Simon

6 Kirsty McColl had a chart hit with the song *A New England*. Who wrote it?

    A Shane McGowan
    B Billy Bragg
    C Ben Elton

7 What was red about the Viking explorer Eric the Red?

    A His nose
    B His hair
    C His bloody sword

8 Where did the Elgin Marbles come from?

    A The Parthenon in Athens
    B The Temple at Delphi
    C Palace of Knossos on Crete

9 What does an exlibrist collect?

    A Books
    B Book plates
    C Old library books

10 In football, how far is the goal line from the penalty spot?

    A 12 feet
    B 12 metres
    C 12 yards

11 What church feast day is traditionally celebrated on 26th December?

    A St Stephen, the first martyr
    B Holy Innocents, the babies King Herod slaughtered
    C No-one's, it's Boxing Day

12 Who is made of sugar, spice and everything nice, plus an accidental spill of Chemical X?

    A Dee Dee (from *Dexter's Lab*)
    B *The Powerpuff Girls*
    C *Superwoman*

1 What was the name of the US space shuttle that exploded shortly after take-off in 1986?

    A Discovery
    B Challenger
    C Columbia

2 What traditional belief caused countrypeople not to pick blackberries after 29th September?

    A Their laxative properties grew greatly after then
    B Unpicked berries meant a good crop next year
    C The devil was said to pee or spit on them on 29th

3 How did the poet Rupert Brooke die in 1915?

    A From septicemia after a mosquito bite
    B From wounds received in battle
    C From an accident on his motorbike

4 Five of the Monopoly players' tokens are a ship, hat, racehorse, boot and car. What is the sixth?

    A An iron
    B An aeroplane
    C A brass bed

5 Who co-writes Texas's songs along with Sharleen Spiteri?

    A Ken McCluskey
    B Johnny McElhone
    C Ally McErlaine

6 If you saw a brigantine, what would you be looking at?

    A A pirate
    B A sailing ship
    C A 58-gallon capacity barrel

7 Edinburgh's mainline railway station is named after a novel by which Scottish writer?

    A Robert Louis Stevenson
    B Walter Scott
    C Irvine Welsh

8 Which year saw the introduction of yellow and red cards in the World Cup?

    A 1962
    B 1966
    C 1970

9 What character did Samuel L. Jackson play in *Star Wars II: Attack of the Clones*?

    A Mace Windu
    B Count Dooku
    C Watto

10 How many legs does a crab have?

    A Ten
    B Eight
    C Six

11 How many years was Nelson Mandela imprisoned before his release in 1990?

    A 22
    B 26
    C 32

12 Which monarch were the Gunpowder Plotters trying to blow up?

    A Henry VIII
    B Elizabeth I
    C James I

A
139

1	B
2	B
3	C
4	B
5	A
6	B
7	B
8	A
9	B
10	C
11	A
12	B

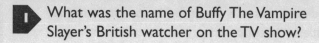

1 What was the name of Buffy The Vampire Slayer's British watcher on the TV show?

    A Ripper Giles
    B Giles Ripper
    C Rupert Giles

2 Christian Orthodox churches that follow the old Julian calendar celebrate Christmas when?

    A 1st January
    B 6th January
    C 7th January

3 Which of these is not a ballet by Tchaikovsky?

    A The Nutcracker
    B Giselle
    C Swan Lake

4 What is the correct term for a cluster of bananas?

    A A bunch
    B A hand
    C A claw

5 When was the Great Train Robbery?

    A 1963
    B 1966
    C 1960

6 Who or what is given the Lev Yashin award at the end of World Cup finals?

    A The goalkeeper voted best in the tournament
    B The referee voted worst in the tournament
    C The side voted best-looking in the tournament

7 How old must a sheep be before its meat is called mutton?

    A Five years
    B Two years
    C One year

8 What is dried ice also known as?

    A Solid H_2O
    B Solid Oxygen
    C Solid Carbon Dioxide

9 Which Israeli Prime Minister's assassination in 1995 damaged the Middle East peace process?

    A Menachem Begin
    B Yitzhak Rabin
    C Yitzhak Shamir

10 What is the name of Mowgli's panther guardian in *The Jungle Book*?

    A Bagheera
    B Baloo
    C Shere Khan

11 Who was the drummer in The Jam?

    A Rick Butler
    B Rick Buckler
    C Rick Belter

12 Which is the only river that flows both north and south of the Equator?

    A The Amazon
    B The Congo
    C The Nile

A
140

1	B
2	C
3	A
4	A
5	B
6	B
7	B
8	C
9	A
10	A
11	B
12	C

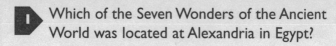

QUESTIONS

142

1 Which of the Seven Wonders of the Ancient World was located at Alexandria in Egypt?

   A The Pharos Lighthouse
   B The Great Pyramid
   C The Statue of Zeus

2 'A family with the wrong members in control'. What was George Orwell describing?

   A England
   B The Conservative Party
   C The royal family

3 What is the county town of Essex?

   A Romford
   B Southend
   C Chelmsford

4 The English club side once known as Newton Heath are now better known as what?

   A Arsenal
   B Manchester United
   C Liverpool

5 Which country owns the Azores islands in the Atlantic Ocean?

   A Spain
   B Portugal
   C France

6 What does the term 'Feng Shui' actually mean?

   A Pleasant space
   B Wind and water
   C Cosmic balance

7 Who developed ARPANET, the precursor to the Internet?

   A The FBI
   B The US Defence Department
   C NATO

8 Who was Simón Bolívar?

   A The first president of Bolivia
   B South America's liberator from Spanish rule
   C A Cuban guerrilla leader

9 How many hobbits were part of the Fellowship of the Ring?

   A One
   B Two
   C Four

10 Which character did *Thunderbirds'* co-creator Sylvia Anderson voice on the series?

   A Tin-Tin
   B Lady Penelope
   C The Hood

11 What was the biggest-selling single of the 1990s?

   A Elton John's *Candle in the Wind 1997*
   B Wet Wet Wet's *Love Is All Around*
   C Bryan Adams' *Everything I Do (I Do It For You)*

12 How many copies did Elton John's *Candle In The Wind 1997* sell around the world?

   A 57 million
   B 35 million
   C 21 million

A
141

1	C
2	C
3	B
4	B
5	A
6	A
7	C
8	C
9	B
10	A
11	B
12	B

1 The national car registration letters 'RU' indicate which country?

    A Russia
    B Burundi
    C Uruguay

2 Husband and wife pair Ronald Reagan and Nancy Davis starred together in which naval movie?

    A *They Were Expendable*
    B *The Russians Are Coming!*
    C *Hellcats Of The Navy*

3 For which Formula 1 team did British champions Damon Hill and Nigel Mansell drive?

    A Williams
    B Jordan
    C Ferrari

4 Who won the Battle of Stamford Bridge in 1066?

    A King Harold II
    B William the Conqueror
    C Harald Hardrada

5 Where did Sherlock Holmes first meet Dr Watson?

    A In the Reading Room of the British Museum
    B At Bart's Hospital in London
    C At their public school

6 Which is the only country to be intersected by both the Equator and one of the tropics?

    A Australia
    B India
    C Brazil

7 Who recorded *Mama Told Me Not To Come* with the Stereophonics in 2000?

    A Lulu
    B Tom Jones
    C Tony Christie

8 Which Ancient Greek is often called the Father of Medicine?

    A Demosthenes
    B Hippocrates
    C Homer

9 Which disease was known as 'The White Plague'?

    A Syphilis
    B Smallpox
    C Tuberculosis

10 How many EU states were in the Euro currency zone when it began in January 2002?

    A Fifteen
    B Twelve
    C Thirteen

11 What did the Royal Navy begin issuing to its sailors in 1795 to protect them against scurvy?

    A Rum
    B Lemon and lime juice
    C Fresh water

12 In Emily Brontë's *Wuthering Heights*, who does Cathy marry?

    A Edgar Linton
    B Lockwood
    C Heathcliff

A
142

1	A
2	A
3	C
4	B
5	B
6	B
7	B
8	B
9	C
10	B
11	A
12	B

1 On which Mediterranean island is the town of Valletta?

   A Sardinia
   B Corsica
   C Malta

2 Who won the first ever World Cup match?

   A France
   B Mexico
   C Uruguay

3 Which clear yellowish fluid makes up 55% of human blood?

   A Water
   B Plasma
   C Bile

4 In which year was *Desert Island Discs* first broadcast?

   A 1942
   B 1952
   C 1962

5 When did England become a republic?

   A 55 BC
   B 1649
   C England has never been a republic

6 How did Tam o' Shanter escape the ghouls chasing him?

   A By crossing running water
   B By holding up a crucifix at them
   C He didn't; they caught him

7 What colour is the bottom stripe on the USA flag?

    A Red
    B White
    C Blue

8 What was Madonna into on her first UK no. 1?

    A The Music
    B The Groove
    C The Holiday

9 The Jesuits were founded in 1534 in Spain. What were they?

    A The torturers of the Spanish Inquisition
    B A secret group aiming at gaining political power
    C A counter-reformation religious order

10 How many cards are there in a Tarot pack?

    A 52
    B 64
    C 78

11 Who played Mad Gerald, Lord Flashheart and Lieutenant Flashheart in the Blackadder series?

    A Ben Elton
    B Rik Mayall
    C Adrian Edmondson

12 If someone were burked, what would happen to them?

    A They would be suffocated
    B They would be cheated by a con man
    C They would be a practical-joke victim

A
143

1   B
2   C
3   A
4   A
5   B
6   C
7   B
8   B
9   C
10   B
11   B
12   A

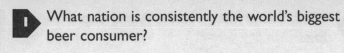

1 What nation is consistently the world's biggest beer consumer?

   A The USA
   B Germany
   C The Czech Republic

2 What was the name of the area of colonial Ireland that was under direct English rule?

   A The Pale
   B The Dáil
   C The Plantation

3 When was the postcode first introduced in Britain?

   A 1940
   B 1959
   C 1968

4 Which artist is considered to be the father of Abstract painting?

   A Miro
   B Pollock
   C Malevich

5 One of the Eurythmics' songs made no. 1 in the 1980s. Which one?

   A *Sweet Dreams*
   B *There Must Be An Angel*
   C *Who's That Girl?*

6 Which writer is thought to have written the first mystery story?

   A Wilkie Collins
   B Edgar Allan Poe
   C Charles Dickens

7 Which country has won the World Cup more times than any other?

  A Brazil
  B Germany
  C Italy

8 What colour of light is shown on the starboard side of a boat or plane?

  A Red
  B Green
  C White

9 What building is home to *Pietà*, Michelangelo's Mary and Christ sculpture?

  A The Louvre, Paris
  B The Prado, Madrid
  C St Peter's Basilica, Rome

10 How many hoops are there in a croquet court?

  A 16
  B 12
  C 10

11 Which character did James Caan play in *The Godfather*?

  A Sonny Corleone
  B Michael Corleone
  C Vito Corleone

12 Who burned Joan of Arc at the stake?

  A The French
  B The English
  C The Catholic Church

A
144

1	**C**
2	**A**
3	**B**
4	**A**
5	**B**
6	**A**
7	**A**
8	**B**
9	**C**
10	**C**
11	**B**
12	**A**

1 Which modern-day country did the Romans call 'Lusitania'?

    A Germany
    B Spain
    C Portugal

2 What powers are conferred on those who kiss the Blarney stone?

    A Eloquent speech
    B The ability to tell truth from fiction
    C The luck of the Irish

3 In which year did Amelia Earhart become the first woman to fly the Atlantic single-handed?

    A 1930
    B 1931
    C 1932

4 Who played Dr Who in the late 70s?

    A Jon Pertwee
    B Peter Davison
    C Tom Baker

5 In the Harry Potter books, what is the name of the wizarding pub in London?

    A The Pickled Slug
    B The Leaky Cauldron
    C The Warlock's Rest

6 At what speed does the Earth rotate around the Sun?

    A 29 km per second
    B 29 km per minute
    C 29 km per hour

7 What does the word 'guerilla' actually mean?

    A Hit and run
    B Little war
    C Person who hides in bushes

8 Which renowned architect designed the famous extension to the Louvre in Paris?

    A Richard Rogers
    B Enric Miralles
    C I.M. Pei

9 Spain have played in six World Cup quarter-finals but have only progressed once. When?

    A 1950
    B 1982
    C 2002

10 From which movie comes the quote, 'Every time a bell rings, an angel gets his wings'?

    A *It's A Wonderful Life*
    B *Dogma*
    C *Angels with Dirty Faces*

11 What Scandinavian band had a hit with *The Sun Always Shines On TV*?

    A Roxette
    B A-Ha
    C Ace Of Base

12 Approximately how many casualties were there after the Battle of the Somme in 1916?

    A 1,265,000
    B 845,000
    C 94,000

1	C
2	A
3	B
4	C
5	B
6	B
7	A
8	B
9	C
10	B
11	A
12	B

1 Which landmark population figure did the Earth pass for the first time in 1999?

- **A** 5,000,000,000
- **B** 6,000,000,000
- **C** 7,000,000,000

2 In 1908, what became the first winter sport ever to be included in the Olympic Games?

- **A** Downhill skiing
- **B** Bobsleigh
- **C** Figure skating

3 What would the word 'chiaroscuro' be used to describe?

- **A** A charred pizza
- **B** A painting with light and dark areas
- **C** A narrow medieval street

4 In which London park is the Serpentine Lake?

- **A** Regents Park
- **B** Hyde Park
- **C** Green Park

5 From which animal does cashmere wool come?

- **A** Sheep
- **B** Goat
- **C** Llama

6 'I'm scared to close my eyes. I'm scared to open them'. Which film is this quote from?

- **A** *The Blair Witch Project*
- **B** *Scream*
- **C** *Nightmare on Elm Street*

7 Which Oscar-winning actress is now one of the top archers in the United States?

    A Sandra Bullock
    B Meryl Streep
    C Geena Davis

8 Who wrote *The Jewel In The Crown* series of novels?

    A Evelyn Waugh
    B Paul Scott
    C E.M. Forster

9 Which Ancient Greek character fulfilled prophecy by killing his father and marrying his mother?

    A Oedipus
    B Jason
    C Hercules

10 What was unusual about Gene Roddenberry's burial in 1997?

    A It took place in space
    B He was buried on the Star Trek lot at Paramount
    C William Shatner gave the funeral oration

11 What is the capital of Madagascar?

    A Maputo
    B Antananarivo
    C Addis Ababa

12 In which sport are the Corbillon Cup and the Swaythling Cup played for?

    A Badminton
    B Lacrosse
    C Table tennis

1 PM Margaret Thatcher was once seen on the Brit Awards singing her favourite song. What was it?

A Maggie May
B How Much Is That Doggy In The Window?
C Tiptoe Through The Tulips

2 Who was Edmund Hillary's companion when he climbed Mount Everest in 1952?

A Sherpa Tenzing Norgay
B George Mallory
C Andrew Irvine

3 What is the rarest winning hand in poker?

A A Royal Flush
B A Full House
C Four of a Kind

4 What is the Israeli parliament called?

A Mossad
B Douma
C Knesset

5 Who was king of the fairies in Shakespeare's *A Midsummer Night's Dream*?

A Oberon
B Puck
C Bottom

6 Agincourt was the final battle in which war?

A The Seven Years' War
B The Hundred Years' War
C The Wars of the Roses

7 What is the capital of Canada?

    A Quebec
    B Ottawa
    C Toronto

8 Which sporting event has its final at the postcode SW19?

    A The FA Cup
    B The Boat Race
    C Wimbledon

9 Who directed *Romeo and Juliet* in 1996?

    A Baz Luhrmann
    B Ridley Scott
    C Sam Raimi

10 If you were a mycologist, what would your speciality be?

    A Diseases of the colon
    B The study of fungi
    C Ancient Greek civilisation

11 What is the Fujita Scale used to measure?

    A Destruction levels of an atomic bomb
    B The intensity of tornadoes
    C The profitability of the Japanese Stock Market

12 In the classic TV series *The Herbs*, what type of animal was Parsley?

    A A dog
    B A parrot
    C A lion

A 147

1	B
2	C
3	B
4	B
5	B
6	A
7	C
8	B
9	A
10	A
11	B
12	C

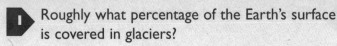

1 Roughly what percentage of the Earth's surface is covered in glaciers?

    A 2%
    B 7%
    C 10%

2 Which former sports presenter left the BBC to follow his spiritual leanings?

    A Frank Bough
    B David Icke
    C Desmond Lynam

3 Who was *Pretty In Pink* in 1986?

    A Ally Sheedy
    B Demi Moore
    C Molly Ringwald

4 Which of the following presidents' heads is not carved into the stone at Mount Rushmore?

    A Lincoln
    B Jefferson
    C Kennedy

5 Who was the next British sprinter after Harold Abrahams to take the 100 metres Olympic gold?

    A Eric Liddell
    B Allan Wells
    C Linford Christie

6 Which of the following was *not* considered by the CIA to assassinate Cuban President Castro?

    A A poisoned wet suit
    B An exploding seashell
    C An anthrax-coated baseball

7 What does a fletcher make?

    A Arrows
    B Barrels
    C Thatched roofs

8 Which band are notorious for peeing and vomiting on stage?

    A Limp Bizkit
    B Slipknot
    C Korn

9 What is the largest island in the world (excluding the continental mass of Australia)?

    A Borneo
    B Greenland
    C New Guinea

10 What is the lightest weight category in boxing?

    A Midget
    B Flyweight
    C Light Flyweight

11 What disease killed the poet John Keats in Rome in 1821?

    A Tuberculosis
    B Malaria
    C Smallpox

12 What is the difference between fruits and vegetables?

    A Fruits have a higher sugar content than vegetables
    B Fruits have or are seeds, but vegetables do not
    C Fruits are more brightly coloured than vegetables

A
148

1	B
2	A
3	A
4	C
5	A
6	B
7	B
8	C
9	A
10	B
11	B
12	C

1 Who did Colin Firth play in the TV dramatisation of *Pride And Prejudice*?

   A Mr Bingley
   B Mr Darcy
   C Mr Bennett

2 What nationality was the Surrealist painter Salvador Dali?

   A Portuguese
   B Spanish
   C Italian

3 What Scottish band had a hit with *Nothing Ever Happens*?

   A Travis
   B Del Amitri
   C Texas

4 What is the venue for the 2008 Olympic Games?

   A London
   B Kuala Lumpur
   C Beijing

5 What are whirling dervishes?

   A A type of tumbleweed found in Arizona
   B Members of a Muslim sect
   C Bush-dwelling Australian marsupials

6 Until the end of the Second World War, what was the name of the Japanese secret police?

   A Thought Police
   B SMERSH
   C Hansei

7 Which one of the following sayings about the Royal Navy is attributed to Winston Churchill?

A Its only achievements are our British freedoms
B Its only certainties were scurvy and an early death
C Its only traditions are rum, sodomy and the lash

8 What do *Treasure Island*, *The Lord Of The Flies* and *Robinson Crusoe* have in common?

A They were all written by Scots
B They were all set on islands
C A cannibal ate a main character in each

9 Which colour of light has the shortest wavelength?

A Blue
B Red
C Yellow

10 Which Scottish football side has the nickname The Bhoys?

A Celtic
B Hearts
C Stranraer

11 What common wonder drug is used to combat pain, fever, arthritis, blood clots and heart attacks?

A Penicillin
B Aspirin
C Paracetamol

12 Which country has the longest coastline in the world?

A Australia
B Russia
C China

1	C
2	B
3	C
4	C
5	B
6	C
7	A
8	B
9	B
10	C
11	A
12	B

1 At 42 years old, who is the oldest player ever to have scored at the World Cup finals?

    A Roger Milla (Cameroon)
    B Uwe Seeler (West Germany)
    C Jan Heintze (Denmark)

2 Who was the first woman ever to win a Best Actress Oscar?

    A Janet Gaynor
    B Mary Pickford
    C Norma Shearer

3 Robbie Williams' *Eternity* was part of a double A-side. What was the other track?

    A *Let Me Entertain You*
    B *Road To Mandalay*
    C *Rock DJ*

4 What was Italian astronomer and scientist Galileo's second name?

    A Galilei
    B Galileo
    C Michelangelo

5 In which book would you find the kingdom of Brobdingnag?

    A *Paradise Lost*
    B *Gulliver's Travels*
    C *The Lord of the Rings*

6 Which is the only line on the London Underground to connect with every other line?

    A Circle
    B District
    C Jubilee

7 Which is the most attention-attracting colour?

    A White
    B Yellow
    C Red

8 If you saw an arabesque demonstrated, what would you expect to see?

    A A checkmate manoeuvre in chess
    B A dressage display in a showring
    C A ballet movement

9 Where was *The Lord Of The Rings* mainly filmed?

    A New Zealand
    B Ireland
    C Austria

10 What music is playing in the background to the first scene of *Trainspotting*?

    A Primal Scream *Trainspotting*
    B New Order *Temptation*
    C Iggy Pop *Lust For Life*

11 Which writer coined the phrase 'Generation X'?

    A Douglas Coupland
    B Don DeLillo
    C Carl Hiaasen

12 Roald Amundsen was the first person to reach the South Pole. Who was the second?

    A Captain Scott
    B Ernest Shackleton
    C Sven Hedin

A
150

1 B
2 B
3 B
4 C
5 B
6 A
7 C
8 B
9 A
10 A
11 B
12 B

307

1 Which Portuguese colony had a third of its population killed after an Indonesian invasion in 1975?

A East Timor
B Mozambique
C Macao

2 What does the zodiac show?

A The star clusters that are visible all night
B A ring of the brightest stars in the night sky
C The path the sun seems to take through the sky

3 Which blood group is the only one that can be given in transfusion to any other blood group?

A O
B A
C B

4 In the region of which modern-day country did Islam originate?

A Israel
B Jordan
C Saudi Arabia

5 What was the name of the spaced-out rabbit in *The Magic Roundabout* TV show?

A Zebedee
B Dylan
C Brian

6 The first-ever World Cup was held in 1930. Which country hosted it?

A Spain
B Germany
C Uruguay

7 How many syllables are there in a Japanese haiku?

    A 17
    B 14
    C 21

8 Eric Carmen had a hit with *All By Myself* in 1976 but who had a hit with it in 1997?

    A Celine Dion
    B Whitney Houston
    C Shania Twain

9 Which medical condition reputedly gave rise to the nursery rhyme, *Ring-a-Roses*?

    A The common cold
    B Bubonic Plague
    C Eczema

10 What is the name of Tony Blair's youngest son?

    A Euan
    B Nicky
    C Leo

11 How was the granite used to build pyramids in Ancient Egypt, transported from the quarries?

    A By barges on the River Nile
    B By oxen pulling carts
    C By slave teams rolling granite slabs on logs

12 Arnold Schwarzenegger played which Batman villain?

    A Two-face
    B Mr Freeze
    C The Riddler

A
151

1 A
2 A
3 B
4 A
5 B
6 C
7 C
8 C
9 A
10 C
11 A
12 A

1 What is Eminem's real name?

A Crispian Mills
B Slim Shady
C Marshall Mathers

2 If you lived in a plutocracy, who would run your government?

A The rich
B The military
C The men

3 How many arms has a squid?

A Eight
B Nine
C Ten

4 Which of these American musicals was NOT written by Rodgers and Hammerstein?

A *The King and I*
B *Carousel*
C *Kismet*

5 At which racecourse is the Derby run?

A Epsom
B Cheltenham
C Derby

6 Who or what was a nabob?

A An ancient Byzantine temple
B A growth caused by restrictive codpieces
C Someone who had made a fortune in India

7 Which Canadian province has Edmonton as its capital?

A Alberta
B Saskatchewan
C Manitoba

8 Jay and Silent Bob first appeared in which Kevin Smith film?

A *Chasing Amy*
B *Clerks*
C *Mallrats*

9 What relation is Scrappy Doo to Scooby Doo?

A His son
B His nephew
C His imaginary friend

10 Which club has won the FA cup more times than any other?

A Manchester United
B Blackburn Rovers
C Tottenham Hotspur

11 What is the Great Red Spot that can be seen on Jupiter?

A A crater on the surface
B A storm in the atmosphere
C A huge mountain

12 Which punk rock band got their only no. 1 hit six years after they had split up?

A Siouxie & The Banshees
B The Sex Pistols
C The Clash

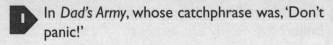

1 In *Dad's Army*, whose catchphrase was, 'Don't panic!'

A Private Fraser
B Corporal Jones
C Captain Mainwaring

2 Why did the play *Playboy of the Western World* cause a riot at Dublin's Abbey Theatre in 1907?

A It featured two men kissing on stage
B The priest in the play was having an affair
C It made mention of a woman's petticoat

3 What are quasars?

A Unstable stars that will soon explode
B Bright galaxies far away, that only look like stars
C Enormous stars with strong gravitational pulls

4 What is the modern name of the former French protectorate of Upper Volta?

A Rwanda
B Democratic Republic of Congo
C Burkina-Faso

5 Name the cat in Disney's film version of *Pinocchio*.

A Figaro
B Galileo
C Mozart

6 Who had a top-ten hit with a song about the famous Ali-Foreman fight, *Rumble In The Jungle*?

A The Fugees
B Johnny Wakelin
C Survivor

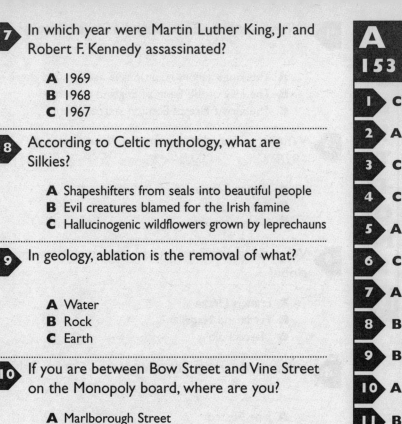

7 In which year were Martin Luther King, Jr and Robert F. Kennedy assassinated?

  A 1969
  B 1968
  C 1967

8 According to Celtic mythology, what are Silkies?

  A Shapeshifters from seals into beautiful people
  B Evil creatures blamed for the Irish famine
  C Hallucinogenic wildflowers grown by leprechauns

9 In geology, ablation is the removal of what?

  A Water
  B Rock
  C Earth

10 If you are between Bow Street and Vine Street on the Monopoly board, where are you?

  A Marlborough Street
  B Old Kent Road
  C Liverpool Street Station

11 Which player has scored most goals in the World Cup finals?

  A Pele
  B Eusebio
  C Gerd Muller

12 What type of instrument is a xylophone?

  A Keyboard
  B Percussion
  C String

1 C
2 A
3 C
4 C
5 A
6 C
7 A
8 B
9 B
10 A
11 B
12 C

1 Why is London's Threadneedle Street famous?

    A The king's tailors traditionally have a shop there
    B The HQ of the Bank of England is there
    C The Great Fire of London started there

2 Whose screen debut came in *Plane Crazy* in 1928?

    A Buster Keaton
    B Popeye
    C Mickey Mouse

3 Who sailed the first ship to circumnavigate the globe?

    A Francis Drake
    B Ferdinand Magellan
    C Marco Polo

4 Who wrote under the pseudonym Currer Bell?

    A Jane Austen
    B Charlotte Brontë
    C Virginia Woolf

5 What words appear on the band across the globe on the Brazilian flag?

    A Ordem e Progresso (Order and Progress)
    B Brasil Para Sempre (Brazil Forever)
    C Mundo Novo (New World)

6 After Communism fell, which Russian city reverted to its original name of St Petersburg?

    A Leningrad
    B Stalingrad
    C Trotskygrad

7 Answer immediately: what is the tenth letter of the alphabet?

A J
B I
C K

8 When was the only time a host country had to qualify for the World Cup finals?

A Uruguay in 1930
B Italy in 1934
C France in 1938

9 In Cleveland, Ohio, it is illegal to operate a vehicle while sitting on another person's what?

A Head
B Knee
C Luggage

10 Tammy Wynette's 1975 hit *D.I.V.O.R.C.E.* was satirised in another hit by which British comedian?

A Jasper Carrot
B Billy Connolly
C Keith Harris and Orville

11 Which Russian ruler was overthrown in the Bolshevik uprising of November 1917?

A Tsar Nicholas II
B Alexander Kerensky
C Leon Trotsky

12 What colour is zinc oxide?

A Grey
B Reddish-brown
C White

A
154

1 B
2 C
3 B
4 C
5 A
6 B
7 B
8 A
9 B
10 A
11 C
12 B

1 Which one of King Arthur's Knights of the Round Table eventually found the Holy Grail?

   A Bedevere
   B Lancelot
   C Galahad

2 The Cristo Rei statue is Rio de Janeiro's most famous landmark. What other city has a copy?

   A Rome
   B Lisbon
   C Madrid

3 What is a bouzouki?

   A A Greek dish of chick peas and rice
   B A long-necked, stringed instrument
   C A long-range gun used in WWI trenches

4 Which former Arsenal player won the Golden Boot in the World Cup in 1998?

   A Thierry Henry (France)
   B Emmanuel Petit (France)
   C Davor Suker (Croatia)

5 What historical event happened at Runnymede in 1215?

   A King John signed Magna Carta
   B The Peasants' Revolt against Richard II began
   C Richard I set out for the first Crusade

6 Who is the lead singer of Blur?

   A Fran Healey
   B Damon Albarn
   C Jarvis Cocker

7 What was cartoon character Hong Kong Phooey's day job?

A Telephone operator
B Janitor
C Karate instructor

8 In *The Lord Of The Rings*, who is the daughter of Elrond, Lord of Rivendell?

A Galadriel
B Arwen
C Lúthien

9 What causes the noise of thunder?

A Several masses of clouds crashing together
B Lightning's rapid heating and expansion of the air
C The sparking of gathering electricity

10 Who was the British Prime Minister at the start of the Second World War?

A Clement Attlee
B Winston Churchill
C Neville Chamberlain

11 All Saints' *Pure Shores* was the theme song for which film?

A *The Beach*
B *Captain Corelli's Mandolin*
C *The Perfect Storm*

12 Which southern US state is known as 'The Peach State'?

A Georgia
B South Carolina
C Tennessee

A
155

1 B
2 C
3 B
4 B
5 A
6 A
7 A
8 A
9 B
10 B
11 B
12 C

317

1 What do a hogshead, a puncheon and a firkin have in common?

A They were traditional measures of beer
B They were dishes served at medieval feasts
C They were traditional measures of land

2 Who sang the opening line of the Band Aid single, *Do They Know It's Christmas*?

A Bono
B Paul Young
C Bob Geldof

3 How many cellos are there in a typical string quartet?

A Four
B One
C None

4 To which pharaoh did the Great Pyramid at Giza belong?

A Ramses II
B Akhenaten
C Khufu

5 Which are normally the three flavours in Neapolitan ice cream?

A Vanilla, raspberry and caramel
B Mint, chocolate and vanilla
C Strawberry, vanilla and chocolate

6 In which British city is the National Railway Museum?

A Crewe
B Doncaster
C York

7 Only one planet in our Solar System spins clockwise; which one is it?

    A Earth
    B Venus
    C Mercury

8 Which martial art is a stylised form of fencing with bamboo staves?

    A Aikido
    B Ninjitsu
    C Kendo

9 How fast is our galaxy thought to be moving through space?

    A 600 km per second
    B 1,045 km per second
    C It isn't moving

10 How long is a marathon (to the nearest mile)?

    A 18
    B 26
    C 40

11 Triassic, Jurassic and Cretaceous are all what?

    A Classes of dinosaurs, based on their chosen diet
    B Three periods in Earth's pre-history
    C Types of pre-historic rock formations

12 How many South American countries share a border with Brazil?

    A Five
    B Eight
    C Ten

1 In Dickens' *Bleak House*, how does Krook meet his maker?

    A He is struck by lightning
    B He is pushed over a cliff
    C He spontaneously combusts

2 What sci-fi series featured Lister, Rimmer and Kryton?

    A *Star Trek: Deep Space Nine*
    B *Red Dwarf*
    C *Babylon 5*

3 Cerberus, three-headed canine guardian of the underworld, was lulled to sleep by whose music?

    A Demeter
    B Eurydice
    C Orpheus

4 Which of these films won the 1977 Best Picture Oscar.

    A *Annie Hall*
    B *Star Wars*
    C *The Goodbye Girl*

5 How much salt does the human body need per day to survive?

    A 1 gram
    B 5 grams (1 teaspoon)
    C None

6 Which Australian ace won the Wimbledon men's singles title four times in the 1960s?

    A Rod Laver
    B John Newcombe
    C Neale Fraser

7 Whose lover was Lady Emma Hamilton?

    A The Duke of Wellington
    B Lord Nelson
    C King Charles II

8 In the song of the same name, where is Heartbreak Hotel?

    A On Fifth and Bell
    B Lonely Street
    C Down on the corner

9 Which jockey has a record thirty Classics victories in his career?

    A Lester Piggott
    B Pat Eddery
    C Frankie Dettori

10 What uncle and nephew have both featured in the *Star Wars* film series?

    A Denis Lawson and Ewan McGregor
    B Alec Guinness and Anthony Daniels
    C Frank Oz and Mark Hamill

11 Who was thought too senile by Britain in 1998 to stand trial for murders in his own country?

    A Radovan Karadzic
    B Idi Amin
    C General Pinochet

12 The Irish flag has three bars of green, white and orange. What does the orange stand for?

    A It represents the Orange, or Protestant people
    B It represents the gold of the leprechauns
    C It was the colour of St Patrick's robes

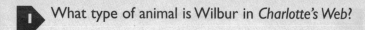

1 What type of animal is Wilbur in *Charlotte's Web*?

A A spider
B A pig
C A mouse

2 Who first said the Earth was spinning through space?

A Ptolemy, the ancient Greek astronomer
B 16th-century astronomer Copernicus
C Galileo, the 17th-century scientist

3 How many points does a dropped goal score in rugby league?

A One
B Two
C Three

4 Whose last words were reputed to be, 'Bugger Bognor!'

A Harold Wilson
B The head of Bognor's tourism department
C George V

5 What was the first team to win the World Cup twice?

A Italy
B Brazil
C Uruguay

6 What are the Wiltshire Horn, the Friesland and the Shropshire?

A Breeds of sheep
B English country dances
C Names of battleships

7 What did Oscar Wilde say that each man does to the thing he loves?

   A Spends it
   B Treasures it
   C Kills it

8 Whose coat did the jester borrow in the Don McLean song *American Pie*?

   A Jack Flash's
   B Buddy Holly's
   C James Dean's

9 What is a virginal?

   A A Roman sooth-sayer
   B A small harpsichord
   C A style of French painting

10 During the British Civil Wars, who or what was the Rump?

   A It was the remains of the British royal family
   B It was a name given to Parliament after a purge
   C It was an affectionate nickname for Cromwell

11 Which is the most highly populated continent?

   A Africa
   B Asia
   C America (N & S)

12 What was the name of the eccentric scientist in the film *Back To The Future*?

   A Doc Tannen
   B Doc Kennedy
   C Doc Brown

1 What was the name of Adolf Hitler's personal guard?

    A The SS
    B The Luftwaffe
    C The SA

2 Which woman has held most Grand Slam tennis titles?

    A Martina Navratilova
    B Billie Jean King
    C Margaret Court

3 Which tree is traditionally associated with death?

    A Holly
    B Yew
    C Willow

4 Approximately how long does it take a garden spider to spin a web?

    A One hour
    B Twelve hours
    C Three days

5 At the Battle of Flodden in 1513, who did the English defeat?

    A The Scots
    B The Welsh
    C The Irish

6 Which late 19th-century French artist is best known for his pictures of ballet dancers?

    A Edgar Degas
    B Auguste Renoir
    C Toulouse-Lautrec

7 Who was the last British governor of Hong Kong?

    A Chris Patten
    B Michael Portillo
    C Peter Mandelson

8 Which Hollywood A-list celebrity appeared in the final episode of *The Fast Show*?

    A Brad Pitt
    B Kevin Spacey
    C Johnny Depp

9 What type of shop traditionally had three balls suspended outside?

    A Butcher's
    B Chemist's
    C Pawnbroker's

10 All life is based on one element. Which one?

    A Oxygen
    B Carbon
    C Radium

11 In the original *Star Wars*, what did Han Solo boast his ship could do in less than 12 parsecs?

    A The Kessel Run
    B The Dagobah Run
    C The Ord Mantell Run

12 In which Shakespearean tragedy do Rosencrantz and Guildenstern appear?

    A *Othello*
    B *King Lear*
    C *Hamlet*

1	B
2	B
3	A
4	C
5	A
6	A
7	C
8	C
9	B
10	B
11	B
12	C

1 How many of his wives outlived Henry VIII?

A None
B One
C Two

2 Who is Dennis the Menace's canine companion?

A Gnasher
B Snowy
C Walter

3 What part of a set of bagpipes is the chanter?

A The bag
B The pipe with finger holes
C The person playing them

4 What is the name of Barbie's boyfriend?

A Paul
B Ken
C Steve

5 From which film does the line, 'You're gonna need a bigger boat' come?

A *Some Like It Hot*
B *Titanic*
C *Jaws*

6 What is the common Indian ingredient ghee?

A Coconut oil
B Clarified butter
C Beef lard

7 What country's flag is the British Blue Ensign with four five-pointed stars in the fly?

   A Australia
   B New Zealand
   C Tonga

8 In which sport would you encounter a bedpost, a six pack, a blow and a cherry?

   A American football
   B Baseball
   C Tenpin bowling

9 If the perimeter of a square is 56 feet, how long is one side?

   A 14 feet
   B 7 feet
   C 28 feet

10 Who said, 'I love Mickey Mouse more than any woman I've ever known'?

   A Donald Duck
   B Walt Disney
   C President Eisenhower

11 In the opera of the same name, who was the Barber Of Seville?

   A Figaro
   B Don Giovanni
   C Giuseppe

12 What is the blood disorder hypotension?

   A Excessive bleeding
   B Low blood pressure
   C High blood pressure

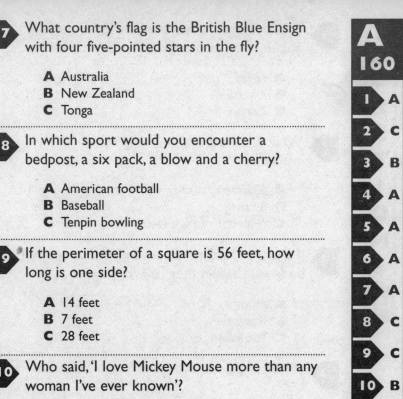

A
160

1 A
2 C
3 B
4 A
5 A
6 A
7 A
8 C
9 C
10 B
11 A
12 C

1 Which impoverished and famine-hit country was once called 'the breadbasket of Africa'?

   A Kenya
   B Zimbabwe
   C Zambia

2 What is a chaparral?

   A A dense area of shrubs and trees
   B A ranch
   C A species of giant cactus

3 If a patient underwent an orchidectomy, what body part would they have removed?

   A An ovary
   B A testicle
   C The palate

4 Which is the largest moon in our solar system?

   A Jupiter's moon Ganymede
   B Saturn's moon Titan
   C The Earth's Moon

5 Which city did Eric Burdon and The Animals come from?

   A New York
   B Newcastle
   C New Orleans

6 What was Tolstoy's original title for *War And Peace*?

   A *Much Ado About Nothing*
   B *The Taming Of The Shrew*
   C *All's Well That Ends Well*

7 In which country was the Auschwitz concentration camp?

    A Germany
    B Czechoslovakia
    C Poland

8 In what sitcom did Judi Dench appear with her real-life husband?

    A *As Time Goes By*
    B *A Fine Romance*
    C *Fresh Fields*

9 Nike was the Greek goddess of what?

    A Leather running sandals
    B Sport
    C Victory

10 Which Formula 1 driver won a record 51 grand prix between 1980 and 1993?

    A Alain Prost
    B Ayrton Senna
    C Niki Lauda

11 What percentage of the world's surface is water?

    A 60%
    B 70%
    C 80%

12 Who is the longest-reigning British monarch?

    A Elizabeth I
    B Elizabeth II
    C Victoria

1	C
2	A
3	B
4	B
5	C
6	B
7	B
8	C
9	A
10	B
11	A
12	B

1 In what stage production could you expect to see Yum-Yum, Ko-Ko and Nanki-Poo?

   A *Teletubbies Live*
   B *The Borstal Boy*
   C *The Mikado*

2 What is added to porcelain to make bone china?

   A Bone ash
   B Ground bone
   C Bone marrow

3 South Africa has two capitals. Where is the country's judicial capital?

   A Bloemfontein
   B Johannesburg
   C Cape Town

4 The number of protons in the nucleus of an atom is known as what?

   A The molecular weight
   B The atomic mass
   C The atomic number

5 Who was Pip's secret benefactor in Dickens' *Great Expectations*?

   A Miss Havisham
   B Jaggers
   C Magwitch

6 From which bridge does the Oxford/Cambridge boat race start?

   A Mortlake
   B Westminster
   C Putney

7 What is the capital city of Vietnam?

    A Hanoi
    B Ho Chi Minh City
    C Da Nang

8 If you were served lumache pasta, what shapes would be on your plate?

    A Crescent-moon shapes
    B Snail-shell shapes
    C Rice-grain shapes

9 The movie *Heavenly Creatures* is based on the life story of which successful mystery writer?

    A Patricia Cornwell
    B Anne Perry
    C P.D. James

10 Who is the victim in a game of Cluedo?

    A Mr Blue
    B Brown the butler
    C Dr Black

11 Which unseeded 17-year-old won the Wimbledon championships in 1985?

    A Stefan Edberg
    B Pat Cash
    C Boris Becker

12 Which father and daughter have both won acting Oscars?

    A John and Angelica Huston
    B Bruce and Gwyneth Paltrow
    C Bruce and Laura Dern

A
162

1	B
2	A
3	B
4	A
5	B
6	C
7	C
8	B
9	C
10	A
11	B
12	C

1 Which Roald Dahl novel included the character Willy Wonka?

    A *Charlie And The Chocolate Factory*
    B *James And The Giant Peach*
    C *Matilda*

2 Anne Boleyn was reputed to have had an extra what?

    A Nipple
    B Finger
    C Navel

3 Who had a hit with *You Took The Words Right Out Of My Mouth* in 1978?

    A Rod Stewart
    B Meatloaf
    C Foreigner

4 Who was the winner of *Big Brother 2*?

    A Kate Lawler
    B Brian Dowling
    C Helen Adams

5 *Canis Lupus* is an animal more commonly known as what?

    A A German Shepherd dog
    B A dingo
    C A wolf

6 Which state hosts the US Masters every year, and staged the Olympic Games in 1996?

    A California
    B Atlanta
    C Louisiana

7 Who was the last Liberal Prime Minister of Britain?

    A Lloyd George
    B Asquith
    C Campbell-Bannerman

8 If someone suffered from nebulaphobia, what would they be afraid of?

    A Fog
    B The stars
    C Asthma inhalers

9 The seven virtues are Faith, Fortitude, Justice, Love, Prudence, Temperance; and what other?

    A Bravery
    B Charity
    C Hope

10 Who was the first woman in space?

    A Sally Ride
    B Svetlana Savitskaya
    C Valentina Tereshkova

11 Who plays the angel Bartelby in the film *Dogma*?

    A Matt Damon
    B Ben Affleck
    C Chris Rock

12 What offence was Al Capone convicted of in 1931?

    A Extortion
    B Murder
    C Tax evasion

A
163

1 C
2 A
3 A
4 C
5 C
6 C
7 A
8 B
9 B
10 C
11 C
12 A

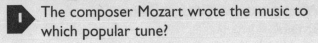

1 The composer Mozart wrote the music to which popular tune?

   A *Happy Birthday To You*
   B *Twinkle, Twinkle, Little Star*
   C *The Sun Has Got His Hat On*

2 How high is the Pyramid of Cheops, or the Great Pyramid?

   A 172 m
   B 147 m
   C 121 m

3 What is the collective name for a group of crows?

   A An exaltation
   B A charm
   C A murder

4 Which English king was the first Prince of Wales?

   A Edward I
   B Edward II
   C Henry VII

5 Actress Hattie Jacques was married to which member of the *Dad's Army* cast?

   A Bill Pertwee
   B Arthur Lowe
   C John Le Mesurier

6 Which political leader 'lost her head' at an art gallery in the summer of 2002?

   A Margaret Thatcher
   B Benazir Bhutto
   C Imelda Marcos

7 Which children's TV character lived at 52 Festive Road?

   A Mr Benn
   B Crystal Tipps
   C Bagpuss

8 From which region of France does wine called claret come?

   A Burgundy
   B Bordeaux
   C Alsace

9 What are the basketball team from Dallas known as?

   A The Mavericks
   B The Cowboys
   C The Texans

10 *Austin Powers 2* featured a cameo appearance by Elvis Costello and which other musician?

   A Madonna
   B Burt Bacharach
   C Paul McCartney

11 When did the Gulf War start?

   A August 1990
   B September 1992
   C July 1989

12 What was the biggest-selling single of the 1980s?

   A *Imagine*
   B *Billie Jean*
   C *Do They Know It's Christmas?*

A
164

1 A
2 B
3 B
4 B
5 C
6 B
7 A
8 A
9 C
10 C
11 B
12 C

1 What does x equal in the following equation: 3(x − 2) = 18?

   A 8
   B -8
   C 7

2 'Mostly harmless'. What was being described here in *The Hitchhiker's Guide to the Galaxy*?

   A Arthur Dent
   B Earth
   C Slartibartfast

3 How old was Henry VIII when he became king?

   A 18
   B 25
   C 29

4 What is the minimum number of points with which you can win a set in tennis?

   A 18
   B 30
   C 24

5 How many keys are there on a standard piano?

   A 102
   B 96
   C 88

6 What cartoon series was created by Trey Parker and Matt Stone?

   A *King Of The Hill*
   B *Beavis And Butthead*
   C *South Park*

7 What is the name given to a young fish?

    A Fry
    B Squab
    C Grig

8 Who expressed their distaste at movie love scenes with 68-year-old men and young actresses?

    A Catherine Zeta Jones
    B Mel Gibson
    C Harrison Ford

9 Which Jewish festival celebrates the Israelites' liberation from slavery in Egypt?

    A Yom Kippur
    B Passover
    C Hanukkah

10 Which Frenchman's final words were, 'Show my head to the people. It is worth seeing'?

    A Danton
    B Robespierre
    C Louis XVI

11 In the 1985 film *Back To The Future*, what was the name of Doc Brown's dog?

    A Marty
    B Einstein
    C Emmet

12 The ancient land of Mesopotamia, with the Tigris and Euphrates rivers, is which modern country?

    A Iran
    B Jordan
    C Iraq

A
165

1 B
2 B
3 C
4 B
5 C
6 A
7 A
8 B
9 A
10 B
11 A
12 C

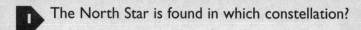
1 The North Star is found in which constellation?

  A Orion The Hunter
  B The Great Bear
  C The Little Bear

2 When Christopher Columbus landed in the Caribbean in 1492, where did he think he was?

  A Japan
  B The East Indies
  C Florida

3 Who composed the opera *Oedipus Rex*?

  A Shostakovich
  B Prokofiev
  C Stravinsky

4 Jamie Lee Curtis is the daughter of which two film stars?

  A Tony Curtis and Janet Leigh
  B Tony Curtis and Tippi Hedren
  C Tony Curtis and Debbie Reynolds

5 What do brogans, pattens and sabots all have in common?

  A They're all types of tartan
  B They're all types of footwear
  C They're all types of trouser

6 Who was the fourth wife of Henry VIII?

  A Catherine Howard
  B Anne of Cleves
  C Jane Seymour

7 What ingredient gives beer its bitter taste?

 A The hops
 B The yeast
 C The alcohol

8 Where did the dodo live?

 A Mauritius
 B Madagascar
 C Mauritania

9 What type of plague was the Black Death?

 A Septemic
 B Pneumonic
 C Bubonic

10 What is the capital of the American state of Idaho?

 A Boise
 B Des Moines
 C Frankfort

11 Which Scots band had a hit in the 80s with *Look Away*?

 A Altered Images
 B Simple Minds
 C Big Country

12 Which 1967 war left Israel with the Gaza Strip, Golan Heights, Sinai Peninsula and West Bank?

 A The Six Day War
 B The Yom Kippur War
 C The Transjordan War

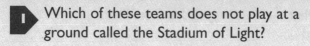

QUESTIONS

168

1 Which of these teams does not play at a ground called the Stadium of Light?

   A Sunderland
   B Benfica
   C Atletico Madrid

2 In ancient times which group of women warriors terrorised North Africa and Asia Minor?

   A Amazons
   B Sarmatians
   C Ephesians

3 What is the heraldic colour sable more commonly known as?

   A Brown
   B Silver
   C Black

4 In what year was the Atlantic first crossed by balloon?

   A 1883
   B 1978
   C The Atlantic has never been crossed by balloon

5 What rock star was a member of both The Yardbirds and Blind Faith?

   A Graham Gouldman
   B Peter Gabriel
   C Eric Clapton

6 What was Lady Chatterley's first name?

   A Charity
   B Constance
   C Cynthia

7 What is the name of the Canadian national anthem?

    A *The Glorious Maple Leaf*
    B *O Canada*
    C *True North*

8 Who hosts Radio 4's *Just a Minute*?

    A Nicholas Parsons
    B Humphrey Lyttleton
    C Clive Anderson

9 At which track is the San Marino Grand Prix held?

    A Monza
    B Magny-Cours
    C Imola

10 Who was the inventor of Polaroid photography?

    A George Eastman
    B Francis Crick
    C Edwin F. Land

11 What would you call a record of the types and numbers of atoms in a molecule?

    A Report log
    B Chemical formula
    C Symbol

12 What did St Augustine pray that God would make him, 'but not yet'?

    A A saint
    B Chaste
    C Sober

A
167

1	C
2	B
3	C
4	A
5	B
6	B
7	A
8	A
9	C
10	A
11	C
12	A

1 Approximately how long has Britain been an island?

   A 10,000 years
   B 65,000 years
   C Britain has always been an island

2 What does the name of the Portuguese popular music style Fado, translate as?

   A Blues
   B Fate
   C Pop

3 If you were served gumbo in the southern US, what would you expect to be eating?

   A A sticky rice cake
   B A fish stew
   C Corn flatbread

4 Who played the father in the 1951 film *Father Of The Bride*?

   A Cary Grant
   B Spencer Tracy
   C Humphrey Bogart

5 Who played the father in the 1991 remake of *Father Of The Bride*?

   A Steve Martin
   B Chevy Chase
   C Bill Murray

6 Hadrian's Wall runs from Wallsend in the east to which town in the west?

   A Norcaster
   B Bowness
   C Carlisle

7 What is the size of the Milky Way, in light years?

A 100,000 light years
B 20,000 light years
C 3,000,000 light years

8 Where is the Republic of Suriname?

A Africa
B Asia
C South America

9 What was the name of Bob Dylan's first album?

A *Bob Dylan*
B *The Freewheelin' Bob Dylan*
C *The Times They Are A-Changin'*

10 Which British city hosted both the 1970 and the 1986 Commonwealth Games?

A Manchester
B Birmingham
C Edinburgh

11 By what more famous name is Nicholas Coppola better known?

A Francis Ford Coppola
B Nicholas Cage
C Emilio Estevez

12 Charles V spoke 'Spanish to God, Italian to women, French to men'. Who did he speak German to?

A His servants
B His lover
C His horse

1 C
2 A
3 C
4 B
5 C
6 B
7 B
8 A
9 C
10 C
11 B
12 B

1 In the *Doctor Who* show, what does TARDIS actually mean?

    A Time And Relative Dimensions In Space
    B Trans-Arc Random Displacement Infinity Ship
    C Time-Adjusted Reality Distortion In Space

2 Who was the last Spaniard to win Wimbledon to date?

    A Arantxa Sanchez-Vicario
    B Juan Carlos Ferrero
    C Conchita Martinez

3 When was the first successful criminal conviction on the basis of fingerprint evidence?

    A 1841
    B 1885
    C 1902

4 Which song did Doris Day sing in the 1956 film *The Man Who Knew Too Much*?

    A *Che Sara Sara*
    B *Secret Love*
    C *Our Day Will Come*

5 How is artist Jerome von Acken better known?

    A Hieronymous Bosch
    B Picasso
    C Rembrandt

6 When was Guy Fawkes arrested in the cellar beneath Parliament?

    A 5th November, 1604
    B 4th November, 1605
    C 5th November, 1606

7 Which of these songs has not been a hit for Rolf Harris?

   A *Stairway to Heaven*
   B *Bohemian Rhapsody*
   C *Purple Haze*

8 What is the second full moon in a month called?

   A Blue Moon
   B Werewolves' Moon
   C Second Moon

9 What is the date of St George's Day?

   A 23rd April
   B 1st April
   C 17th April

10 Officially, how long is a jiffy?

   A 5 seconds
   B 0.5 second
   C 0.01 second

11 Who created private detective Mike Hammer?

   A Raymond Chandler
   B Dashiell Hammet
   C Mickey Spillane

12 Which modern opera does the song *Mack the Knife* come from?

   A *Life With An Idiot*
   B *The Threepenny Opera*
   C *Nixon in China*

1	A
2	B
3	B
4	B
5	A
6	B
7	A
8	C
9	A
10	C
11	B
12	C

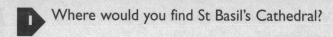

1 Where would you find St Basil's Cathedral?

    A Moscow
    B Rome
    C Istanbul

2 Who had 'the face that launched a thousand ships'?

    A Elizabeth I
    B Lady Cunard
    C Helen of Troy

3 In the 1992 film of *Bram Stoker's Dracula*, who played Dracula?

    A Gary Oldman
    B Kenneth Branagh
    C Tim Roth

4 Which was the first London underground line to open in 1863?

    A Metropolitan
    B Circle
    C District

5 Which former top SS officer did the Israelis snatch from hiding in Argentina in 1960?

    A Josef Mengele
    B Adolf Eichmann
    C Herman Hesse

6 Which country's flag is plain green, with no designs or emblems?

    A Lebanon
    B Liberia
    C Libya

7 Which Midlands football club had the first all-seated stadium in England?

    A Birmingham City
    B Wolves
    C Coventry City

8 In Roman numerals, which number is represented by the letters DCLVI?

    A 5,504
    B 656
    C 96

9 Which of the following comes immediately after matins in the monastic day?

    A Lauds
    B Vespers
    C Compline

10 What is German weizen beer?

    A Wheat beer
    B White beer
    C Beer-and-schnapps cocktail

11 If you added all the numbers from 1 to 100 consecutively, what would you get?

    A 6428
    B 5050
    C 4892

12 The ship *Cutty Sark* was a tea clipper. What does its name mean?

    A The dancing ghoul
    B The fine whisky
    C The short skirt

**A
170**

1	A
2	C
3	C
4	A
5	A
6	B
7	C
8	A
9	A
10	C
11	C
12	B

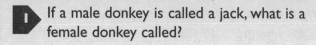

Q U E S T I O N S

172

1 If a male donkey is called a jack, what is a female donkey called?

    A A jill
    B A joan
    C A jenny

2 What colour were the eyes sung about by The Beautiful South in 1992?

    A Blue
    B Black
    C Red

3 Which Hogwarts house is home to Hermione Granger?

    A Ravenclaw
    B Hufflepuff
    C Gryffindor

4 Any month that starts on a Sunday will have what?

    A A full moon
    B A Friday the 13th
    C A special papal blessing

5 If you are born on 1st January, what is your zodiac sign?

    A Capricorn
    B Aquarius
    C Sagittarius

6 'It would be positive relief to dig him up and throw stones at him', said G.B. Shaw of whom?

    A Oscar Wilde
    B William Shakespeare
    C Karl Marx

7 Which super-hero from Eternia did Prince Adam become?

    A Orko
    B He-Man
    C Man-At-Arms

8 What musical sees Seymour fighting off the attentions of Audrey II?

    A *Little Shop of Horrors*
    B *Grease*
    C *Kiss Me, Kate*

9 How many points are awarded to a Formula 1 Grand Prix winner?

    A 15
    B 12
    C 10

10 What did the writer James Joyce call 'the centre of paralysis'?

    A The Catholic Church
    B Dublin
    C His teaching job

11 Which chemical element does the abbreviation Co represent?

    A Copper
    B Cobalt
    C Chlorine

12 Disease, Want, Ignorance and Squalor were four of the ills the Welfare State took on. What was the fifth?

    A Debauchery
    B Idleness
    C Illiteracy

1 In 1959, who invented the hovercraft?

   A Christopher Cockerell
   B Frank Whittle
   C Wallace Carruthers

2 Which player won Wimbledon twice, with an eight-year gap between victories?

   A Stefan Edberg
   B Jimmy Connors
   C Boris Becker

3 'An offensive exhibition of boorishness and vulgarity'. What American icon was being described?

   A Madonna
   B Abraham Lincoln
   C Henry Ford

4 What is the commonest male first name in the world?

   A Muhammad
   B John
   C James

5 How many pedals are there on a grand piano?

   A None
   B One
   C Three

6 Which Brontë sister wrote *Wuthering Heights*?

   A Anne
   B Emily
   C Charlotte

7 Frank Sinatra appeared in twenty films during the 1950s. Which of these was not one of them?

    A *The Manchurian Candidate*
    B *From Here to Eternity*
    C *Guys And Dolls*

8 On *Star Trek: The Next Generation*, what was the name of Captain Picard's fish?

    A Burton
    B Stanley
    C Livingston

9 The first mission to Mars, in 1962, was a USSR one. What was it called?

    A Mars 1
    B Mariner 1
    C Zond 1

10 What was the Tin Lizzie?

    A A 1970s pop band
    B A prototype canning machine
    C The nickname of an early car

11 How much ground had the British won by the end of the four-month Battle of the Somme in 1916?

    A Approximately fifty miles
    B Approximately five miles
    C Approximately ten feet

12 Where does Zinfandel wine come from?

    A USA
    B Chile
    C New Zealand

A
172

1	C
2	C
3	C
4	B
5	A
6	B
7	B
8	A
9	C
10	B
11	B
12	B

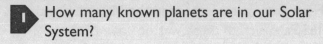

1 How many known planets are in our Solar System?

    A Nine
    B Ten
    C Eleven

2 According to Lloyd George, to succeed in politics you must keep what firmly under control?

    A Your libido
    B Your conscience
    C Your imagination

3 Which classic fantasy series features a wizard called Ged?

    A *The Dark is Rising* series
    B *The Lord Of The Rings*
    C *The Earthsea Trilogy*

4 In the Italian Serie A league, two teams play at the Stadio Delle Alpi. Who are they?

    A Internazionale Milan and AC Milan
    B Roma and Lazio
    C Juventus and Turin

5 In the original *Star Wars*, who is the bounty hunter Han Solo blasts in Mos Eisley cantina?

    A Bossk
    B Boba Fett
    C Greedo

6 What group went their separate ways on Boxing Day 2001?

    A The Spice Girls
    B Steps
    C Five

7 How many guests attended the March Hare's Tea Party?

    A Two
    B Four
    C Seven

8 Which reformer's picture appears on the back of the £5 note issued in 2002?

    A Elizabeth Fry
    B William Wilberforce
    C Sylvia Pankhurst

9 Ricky Martin appeared on which daytime American soap before he shot to pop stardom?

    A *Days Of Our Lives*
    B *General Hospital*
    C *The Bold And The Beautiful*

10 How is the date of Easter calculated?

    A Sunday after the full moon after spring equinox
    B Sunday after Septuagesima
    C It's a secret, kept in an ancient text in the Vatican

11 What is Donald Duck's middle name?

    A Fauntleroy
    B D'Angelo
    C Davidson

12 In the children's TV show *Captain Scarlet*, what are the women fighter pilots called?

    A The Rainbows
    B The Spectrums
    C The Angels

A
173

1 **A**
2 **B**
3 **B**
4 **A**
5 **C**
6 **B**
7 **A**
8 **C**
9 **A**
10 **C**
11 **B**
12 **A**

1 What birds would be given the collective term 'an ostentation of'?

   A Eagles
   B Peafowl
   C Swans

2 Which country did Celine Dion represent in the Eurovision Song Contest?

   A France
   B Switzerland
   C Israel

3 What is the capital of Brazil?

   A Rio de Janeiro
   B São Paolo
   C Brasília

4 In golf, what is an albatross?

   A Three strokes under par at a hole
   B Three strokes over par at a hole
   C Where a player loses their ball completely

5 Who was the British prime minister at the start of the First World War?

   A Balfour
   B Asquith
   C Lloyd George

6 'So far as I am concerned, they are lower than vermin'. Who was speaking about the Tory Party?

   A Aneurin Bevan
   B Tony Blair
   C Winston Churchill

7 Where does Mateus Rose wine come from?

    A California
    B Australia
    C Portugal

8 Which city is currently home to the Mona Lisa?

    A Rome
    B Paris
    C Madrid

9 Why is the planet Venus hotter than the planet Mercury?

    A Venus is closer to the Sun
    B There are boiling lava streams on Venus
    C Mercury has no atmosphere, but Venus does

10 One member of ABBA was not born in Sweden. Which one?

    A Agnetha
    B Benny
    C Frida

11 Who was the toff who had his own strip in *The Beano* comic?

    A Lord Haw-Haw
    B Lord Fauntleroy
    C Lord Snooty

12 Who was the mother of Henry VIII's only son?

    A Jane Seymour
    B Anne Boleyn
    C Catherine Parr

A 174

1 A
2 B
3 C
4 C
5 C
6 B
7 B
8 A
9 B
10 A
11 A
12 C

1 Who replaced Siobhan Fahey when she left Bananarama in 1987?

A Jacqui O'Sullivan
B Keren Woodward
C Belinda Carlisle

2 Who was *Time* magazine's Man Of The Year in 1938?

A Neville Chamberlain
B Franklin D. Roosevelt
C Adolf Hitler

3 In *The Hitchhiker's Guide to the Galaxy*, what is the name of the tennis-shoe-shaped spaceship?

A The Infinite Improbability Drive
B The Heart of Gold
C The White Flash

4 Which one of the following literary figures was also an Irish Senator?

A Samuel Beckett
B Sean O'Casey
C W.B. Yeats

5 According to the Book of Genesis, what did God create first?

A Heaven and Earth
B Water
C Light

6 How did Celtic beat Benfica in 1969 to go on to the European Cup Final the following year?

A They won 8-7 on aggregate
B They won a penalty shoot-out 5-0
C They won on the toss of a coin

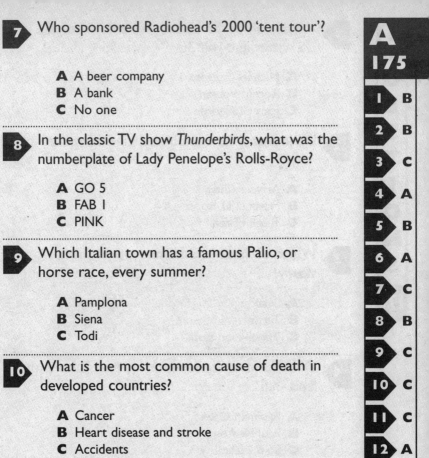

7 Who sponsored Radiohead's 2000 'tent tour'?

    A A beer company
    B A bank
    C No one

8 In the classic TV show *Thunderbirds*, what was the numberplate of Lady Penelope's Rolls-Royce?

    A GO 5
    B FAB I
    C PINK

9 Which Italian town has a famous Palio, or horse race, every summer?

    A Pamplona
    B Siena
    C Todi

10 What is the most common cause of death in developed countries?

    A Cancer
    B Heart disease and stroke
    C Accidents

11 Where is most of the Earth's fresh water found?

    A In the world's rivers
    B In the polar icecaps
    C In underground rivers and lakes

12 What are Gargantua and Pantagruel?

    A Stars in the constellation of Orion
    B Ingredients used in medieval dishes
    C Characters in a literary satire

A
175

1	B
2	B
3	C
4	A
5	B
6	A
7	C
8	B
9	C
10	C
11	C
12	A

1 'A triumph of the embalmer's art'. Who was US writer and wit Gore Vidal talking about?

  A Michael Jackson
  B Ronald Reagan
  C Joan Crawford

2 Darjeeling, Assam and Yunnan are all what?

  A Areas in India
  B Natural lakes
  C Types of tea

3 Which of these land animals moves most slowly?

  A Snail
  B Turtle
  C Three-toed sloth

4 What former Housemartin hit the charts with *Praise You*?

  A Norman Cook
  B Paul Heaton
  C Stan Cullimore

5 When was the world's first successful organ transplant?

  A 1954 in Boston
  B 1967 in Cape Town
  C 1973 in London

6 Ancient Chinese artists never painted one part of women's bodies in their pictures. Which part?

  A Face
  B Fingernails
  C Feet

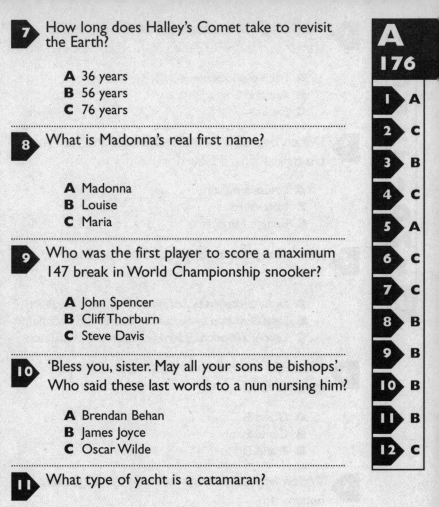

7 How long does Halley's Comet take to revisit the Earth?

    A 36 years
    B 56 years
    C 76 years

8 What is Madonna's real first name?

    A Madonna
    B Louise
    C Maria

9 Who was the first player to score a maximum 147 break in World Championship snooker?

    A John Spencer
    B Cliff Thorburn
    C Steve Davis

10 'Bless you, sister. May all your sons be bishops'. Who said these last words to a nun nursing him?

    A Brendan Behan
    B James Joyce
    C Oscar Wilde

11 What type of yacht is a catamaran?

    A A yacht with two engines
    B A yacht with two masts
    C A yacht with two hulls

12 Who played Lieutenant Uhura in the original *Star Trek* series?

    A Walter Koenig
    B George Takei
    C Nichelle Nicholls

A
176

1 **A**
2 **C**
3 **B**
4 **C**
5 **A**
6 **C**
7 **C**
8 **B**
9 **B**
10 **B**
11 **B**
12 **C**

1 Who sang England's official 2002 World Cup song?

    A Baddiel and Skinner
    B Ant and Dec
    C Fat Les

2 Which one of Dr Who's assistants married the biologist Richard Dawkins?

    A Louise Jameson
    B Lalla Ward
    C Bonnie Langford

3 What does the acronym LASER stand for?

    A Light Absorption by Stimulated Emission of Radiation
    B Light Alteration by Stimulated Emission of Radiation
    C Light Amplification by Stimulated Emission of Radiation

4 What are the only two musical notes which have no flats?

    A G and B
    B C and F
    C A and D

5 Which famous writer wrote *Chitty Chitty Bang Bang*?

    A Ian Fleming
    B Roald Dahl
    C Enid Blyton

6 The largest bicycle ever was 22.24m long with a wheel diameter of 3.05m. What was it called?

    A Big Boy
    B Frankencycle
    C The Road Roller

7 Who said, 'I don't know anything about music. In my line, you don't have to'?

    A Frank Sinatra
    B Elvis Presley
    C Des O'Connor

8 General Gordon died in the siege of Khartoum in 1885. In which modern country is Khartoum?

    A Syria
    B Ethiopia
    C Sudan

9 What kind of fairy is a brownie?

    A A wish-fulfilling elf that appears by magic
    B A useful fairy that did household chores at night
    C A water-spirit that lures travellers to their doom

10 Who scored a hat-trick in England's 1966 World Cup final win over Germany?

    A Bobby Moore
    B Bobby Charlton
    C Geoff Hurst

11 Which cookery writer's successful book on baking is called *How To Be A Domestic Goddess*?

    A Delia Smith
    B Clarissa Dickson-Wright
    C Nigella Lawson

12 How long does it take light from the Sun to reach the Earth?

    A 8.3 seconds
    B 8.3 minutes
    C 8.3 hours

1	B
2	C
3	A
4	A
5	A
6	C
7	C
8	A
9	B
10	A
11	C
12	C

1 In heraldry, if a beast on a coat of arms is described as 'trippant', what would it be doing?

   A Standing on one leg
   B Running
   C Falling over

2 Sr is the chemical symbol for what?

   A Tin
   B Strontium
   C Silver

3 Playwright Arthur Miller wrote a screenplay for his then wife, Marilyn Monroe. What was it?

   A *The Misfits*
   B *Some Like It Hot*
   C *Gentlemen Prefer Blondes*

4 In which extreme sport is the camera operator in almost as much danger as the athlete?

   A Freestyle moto-X
   B Speed climbing
   C Skysurfing

5 Who played Michelangelo in the 1965 film, *The Agony And The Ecstasy*?

   A Charlton Heston
   B Tony Curtis
   C Kirk Douglas

6 Why was the herb tansy considered special by the ancient Greeks and Romans?

   A It could cover all unpleasant household smells
   B It was grown at the doors of conquering generals
   C It was regarded as a symbol of immortality

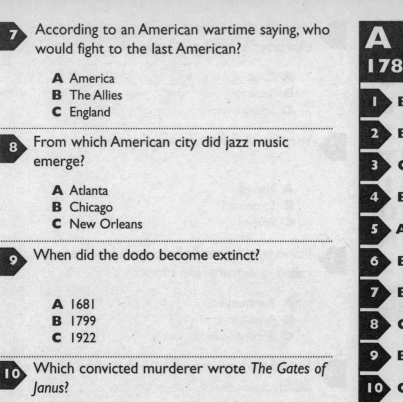

7 According to an American wartime saying, who would fight to the last American?

    A America
    B The Allies
    C England

8 From which American city did jazz music emerge?

    A Atlanta
    B Chicago
    C New Orleans

9 When did the dodo become extinct?

    A 1681
    B 1799
    C 1922

10 Which convicted murderer wrote *The Gates of Janus*?

    A Peter Sutcliffe
    B Dennis Nielsen
    C Ian Brady

11 How old is Bart Simpson?

    A Eight
    B Nine
    C Ten

12 The world's first speed limit, of 2 mph, was introduced in Britain. What was the date?

    A 1921
    B 1894
    C 1865

A
178

1 B
2 B
3 C
4 B
5 A
6 B
7 B
8 C
9 B
10 C
11 C
12 B

1 What is the name of the cat owned by cartoon character Hong Kong Phooey?

    A Chop
    B Spot
    C Suey

2 What nationality was the artist Rubens?

    A Flemish
    B Swiss
    C French

3 In America it is called a sidewalk. What is it called in Britain?

    A A pavement
    B A lane
    C A cul-de-sac

4 Which was the first British ship to send out an SOS?

    A The *Lusitania*
    B The *Titanic*
    C The *Hampshire*

5 What is the first book in Philip Pullman's acclaimed trilogy *His Dark Materials*?

    A *The Amber Spyglass*
    B *Northern Lights*
    C *The Subtle Knife*

6 Who wrote the musical *The Beautiful Game* with Andrew Lloyd Webber?

    A Ben Elton
    B Tim Rice
    C Elton John

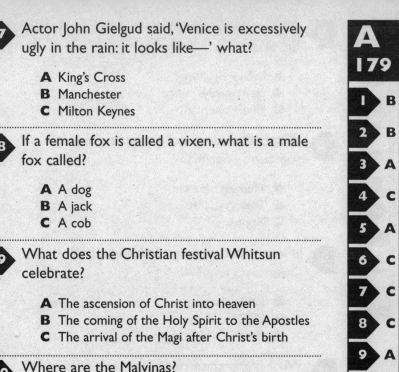

7 Actor John Gielgud said, 'Venice is excessively ugly in the rain: it looks like—' what?

   A King's Cross
   B Manchester
   C Milton Keynes

8 If a female fox is called a vixen, what is a male fox called?

   A A dog
   B A jack
   C A cob

9 What does the Christian festival Whitsun celebrate?

   A The ascension of Christ into heaven
   B The coming of the Holy Spirit to the Apostles
   C The arrival of the Magi after Christ's birth

10 Where are the Malvinas?

   A The Indian Ocean
   B The South Pacific
   C The South Atlantic

11 Why does it take longer to fly from east to west, than from west to east?

   A Because of the pull of Earth's magnetic fields
   B Because upper-atmosphere winds blow west-east
   C Because you fly into the sun's rays as you go east

12 What was American political reformer Malcolm X's original surname?

   A Small
   B Little
   C Short

A
179

1	B
2	B
3	A
4	C
5	A
6	C
7	C
8	C
9	A
10	C
11	C
12	C

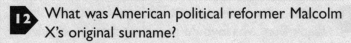

1 Who provides the voice of Sideshow Bob in *The Simpsons*?

A Kelsey Grammer
B David Hyde-Pearce
C John Mahoney

2 What effect does being in space have on someone's height?

A They get shorter
B They get taller
C None

3 In which year was the Falklands War?

A 1982
B 1983
C 1984

4 What is the state capital of Virginia?

A Lincoln
B Dover
C Richmond

5 Whose character is Lord Peter Wimsey?

A Agatha Christie
B Dorothy L. Sayers
C P.G. Wodehouse

6 If you were served the traditional Scottish dish Black Bun, what would you expect to be eating?

A Roast rabbit
B Fruit cake
C Blood sausage

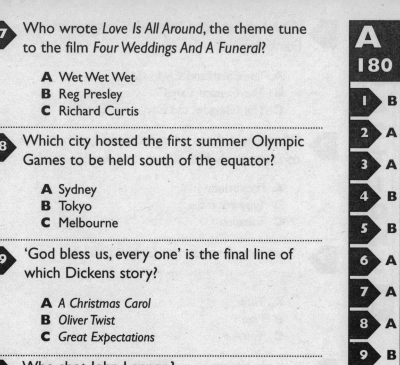

7 Who wrote *Love Is All Around*, the theme tune to the film *Four Weddings And A Funeral*?

   A Wet Wet Wet
   B Reg Presley
   C Richard Curtis

8 Which city hosted the first summer Olympic Games to be held south of the equator?

   A Sydney
   B Tokyo
   C Melbourne

9 'God bless us, every one' is the final line of which Dickens story?

   A *A Christmas Carol*
   B *Oliver Twist*
   C *Great Expectations*

10 Who shot John Lennon?

   A Mark Chapman
   B John Hinckley
   C John Wilkes Booth

11 In Britain, which institution is sometimes called the Fourth Estate?

   A Church of England
   B The monarchy
   C The press

12 How many hairs are there on the average human adult body?

   A 50,000
   B 500,000
   C 5,000,000

A 180

1	B
2	A
3	A
4	B
5	B
6	A
7	A
8	A
9	B
10	C
11	B
12	B

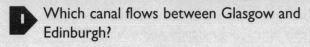

1 Which canal flows between Glasgow and Edinburgh?

    A The Forth and Clyde Canal
    B The Central Canal
    C The Glasgow and Edinburgh Canal

2 Sherlock Holmes wrote a monograph on how to distinguish 140 different types of what?

    A Footprints
    B Typewriters
    C Tobacco

3 What was Cronos the Greek god of?

    A Time
    B Fate
    C The Air

4 Irish playwright Sean O'Faolain said, 'An Irish queer is a fellow who prefers women to—' what?

    A Men
    B Drink
    C Religion

5 What was novelist Fay Weldon's previous profession?

    A Journalist
    B Teacher
    C Copywriter

6 When was Tudor martyr Thomas More canonised?

    A 1735
    B 1835
    C 1935

7 Whose arch-enemy is the evil monkey Mojo Jojo?

    A Dexter
    B The Powerpuff Girls
    C Courage The Cowardly Dog

8 Who became British football's most expensive signing when he joined Manchester Utd in 2002?

    A Les Ferdinand
    B Rio Ferdinand
    C Richey Ferdinand

9 Who wrote the novel *Trainspotting*?

    A Iain Banks
    B Irvine Welsh
    C Christopher Brookmyre

10 How much gas does the average adult pass in a day?

    A 600 ml
    B 1.3 litres
    C 2 litres

11 Old Rowley was a nickname of Charles II. Where was the name taken from?

    A The name of his favourite stallion
    B His nickname for Nell Gwynne
    C A village where he was sheltered while on the run

12 Who wrote for other artists, *Manic Monday*, *Nothing Compares 2 U* and *I Feel For You*?

    A Michael Jackson
    B Prince
    C Trevor Horne

1 Who was Danny in the original London production of *Grease*?

    A Matthew Broderick
    B Richard Gere
    C John Travolta

2 Cars from which country can be recognised by the letters 'FR'?

    A The Faroe Islands
    B Finland
    C France

3 What was described as 'the only country where "academic" is regularly used as a term of abuse'?

    A Australia
    B Turkey
    C England

4 What was the name of Dr Who's pet?

    A KITT
    B K-9
    C Lassie

5 Name the only act to have three UK Christmas number ones in the 1990s.

    A Spice Girls
    B Boyzone
    C Take That

6 Which English side was the first to win the treble of league, cup and European Cup?

    A Liverpool
    B Nottingham Forest
    C Manchester United

7 Who founded the Jesuits, the Catholic Church's counter-Reformation front line?

    A Ignatius Loyola
    B Padre Pio
    C Francis Xavier

8 How many players are there in an ice-hockey team?

    A Seven
    B Nine
    C Eleven

9 Of which president did Lyndon Johnson say, 'He couldn't walk and chew gum at the same time'?

    A John F. Kennedy
    B Gerald Ford
    C Ronald Reagan

10 Which civilisation had its home in the Andes of Peru?

    A Mayans
    B Incas
    C Aztecs

11 What is the first book in Lewis Grassic Gibbon's trilogy *A Scots Quair*?

    A Cloud Howe
    B Sunset Song
    C Grey Granite

12 What was the title of Bill Bryson's best-selling book of his travels around Britain?

    A *Neither Here Nor There*
    B *Mother Tongue*
    C *Notes From A Small Island*

A

182

1	A
2	C
3	A
4	B
5	C
6	C
7	B
8	B
9	B
10	A
11	A
12	B

1 Who became a Pop Idol in 2002?

A Gareth Gates
B Darius Danesh
C Will Young

2 Who succeeded David Vine as host of BBC's *A Question of Sport*?

A David Coleman
B Sue Barker
C John Inverdale

3 Which symphony was Beethoven's last?

A Ninth
B Tenth
C Eighth

4 How is Viscount Stansgate better known?

A Edward Heath
B Tony Benn
C Denis Healey

5 St Jude is the patron saint of what?

A Textile workers
B Traitors
C Hopeless causes

6 How did Oscar Wilde's character Dorian Gray keep his youthful looks?

A He traded his soul with the Devil to stay young
B He took great care of his appearance
C He had a painting which aged while he did not

7 'Destitute of humour, vivacity, or the capacity of enjoyment'. Who was Charles Dickens speaking of?

- **A** Germans
- **B** Australians
- **C** Americans

8 When did TV cat *Bagpuss* first come to life?

- **A** 1974
- **B** 1969
- **C** 1976

9 Portuguese sides won the European Cup three times. Benfica did it twice; who was the other?

- **A** FC Porto
- **B** Sporting Lisbon
- **C** Boavista

10 Why was the Regency figure Beau Brummell famous?

- **A** He joined the Foreign Legion and became a hero
- **B** He was the most fashionable man of his day
- **C** He was architect of the Royal Pavilion at Brighton

11 One of the six murder weapons used in Cluedo is an everyday tool. What is it?

- **A** The spanner
- **B** The hammer
- **C** The screwdriver

12 Who had a hit with *Under the Bridge* in 1998?

- **A** Red Hot Chili Peppers
- **B** All Saints
- **C** Crowded House

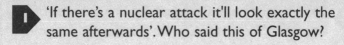

1 'If there's a nuclear attack it'll look exactly the same afterwards'. Who said this of Glasgow?

   A Prince Philip
   B Margaret Thatcher
   C Billy Connolly

2 What nationality was poet and painter Dante Gabriel Rossetti?

   A Portuguese
   B English
   C Italian

3 On which island are Carisbrooke Castle, Osborne House and Black Gang Chine?

   A Isle of Wight
   B Isle of Man
   C Isle of Sheppey

4 Who played Arthur Daley in *Minder*?

   A Dennis Waterman
   B George Cole
   C David Jason

5 In which year was the Battle of Waterloo?

   A 1805
   B 1810
   C 1815

6 What is pâté de foie gras made from?

   A The testicles of a young bullock
   B The liver of a force-fed goose
   C The flesh of a calf under six months old

7 Which Tory politician appeared in a Ribena ad as a child?

   A Norman Tebbitt
   B Michael Howard
   C Michael Portillo

8 Who was the first player to score a hat-trick in a World Cup Final?

   A Gerd Muller
   B Pele
   C Geoff Hurst

9 What is a banshee?

   A A female spirit who wails when death is coming
   B A female leprechaun who often plays a tin whistle
   C A phantom who haunts the countryside at dusk

10 Including the cue ball, how many balls are used in snooker?

   A 17
   B 20
   C 22

11 In 1797 a London man was fined £50 for wearing 'a tall structure of shining lustre'. What was it?

   A The world's first waterproof raincoat
   B The world's first umbrella
   C The world's first top hat

12 What was Blondie's first UK hit single?

   A *Picture This*
   B *Sunday Girl*
   C *Denis*

A
184

1 C
2 A
3 A
4 B
5 C
6 C
7 C
8 A
9 A
10 B
11 A
12 B

1 With what record label did Bob Marley do most of his recording?

    A Island Records
    B Chrysalis
    C Stiff

2 Who played Mark Renton in the 1996 film *Trainspotting*?

    A Jonny Lee Miller
    B Robert Carlyle
    C Ewan McGregor

3 Why was Mexican ruler Montezuma famous?

    A He had 22 children, all of whom were rulers too
    B He built more pyramids than any other ruler
    C He was the last leader of the Aztec kingdom

4 Who was Britain's first million-pound footballer?

    A Trevor Francis
    B Kevin Keegan
    C Kenny Dalglish

5 Who did Pope John Paul succeed in 1978?

    A John XXIII
    B Paul VI
    C Pius XII

6 What was said to have been the food of the Greek gods?

    A Ambrosia
    B Birds' eyes
    C Golden fleece

7 Who won the Eurovision Song Contest twice for Ireland?

   A Johnny Logan
   B Dana
   C Dana International

8 Who won the Tour de France in 2002?

   A Bradley McGee
   B Lance Armstrong
   C Jan Ullrich

9 Which anti-smoking campaigner was the earliest recorded in print?

   A Walter Raleigh
   B King James I
   C William Shakespeare

10 Where do Dr Who's adversaries the Daleks come from?

   A Skaro
   B Skarfayz
   C Skarey

11 If you were sitting on Arthur's Seat, where would you be?

   A Edinburgh
   B Tintagel
   C Glastonbury

12 Which American President said 'I know the human being and fish can coexist peacefully'?

   A George W. Bush
   B Ronald Reagan
   C Gerald Ford

A
185

1	C
2	B
3	A
4	B
5	C
6	B
7	C
8	C
9	A
10	C
11	C
12	C

And the answers to the back cover questions:

A
A
B
C